Emerging With Wings

A True Story of Lies, Pain, And The LOVE that Heals

Danielle Bernock

Media

This book is based upon true events and the author's perception of them. Many events in the author's life have been left out of the story for the sake of brevity or to protect personal privacies. The information provided is designed to provide helpful information on the subjects discussed. The ideas and suggestions in this book are not intended as a substitute for consulting with licensed professionals. Neither the author nor the publisher shall be liable or responsible for any loss, injury, or damage allegedly arising from any information or suggestion in this book. Our views and rights are the same: You are responsible for your own choices, actions, and results. References are provided for informational purposes only and readers should be aware that the websites listed in this book may change.

Cover and interior design by Danielle Bernock and Jessica Litinas

Photos © Danielle Bernock

Lyrics for *"Honesty"* and *"Just Come In"* from the album *"Immigrants Daughter"* used courtesy of Margaret Becker. Lyrics from *"Holy, Holy, Holy (Nicaea)"* and *"Jesus Loves Even Me (Gladness)"* are Public Domain.

Text from Vocabulary.com (http://www.vocabulary.com/), Copyright ©1998-2014 Thinkmap, Inc. All rights reserved. Used by permission.

Unless otherwise identified, scripture references and quotations are from the King James Version of the Bible. Public Domain. Scripture quotations marked (NLT) are taken from the Holy Bible, New Living Translation, copyright © 1996. Used by permission of Tyndale House Publishers, Inc., Wheaton, Illinois 60189. All rights reserved.

ISBN 978-0-9961033-1-2   4F Media - *"Faith Family Friends Freedom"*

SECOND EDITION

With All my heart to

The Love who heard my silent cries,

collected my tears & gave me My Rainbow.

May the Son shine!

Table of Contents

Endorsements

"Emerging with Wings" is a thought-provoking book that examines the mega concepts of good and evil, of truth, lies, pain and the healing power of love. Danielle Bernock discusses how even our most minor day-to-day decisions can change and even transform our lives. While her topics are "deep," there's no need to have majored in philosophy or even studied the great philosophers like Soren Kierkegaard or John Locke to understand her thesis. Danielle examines the major CONCEPTS of validation, personal freedom and love in simple, down-to-earth language, pulling examples from her own life to illustrate her points.

ANNE L. HOLMES
"BOOMER IN CHIEF"
THE NATIONAL ASSOCIATION OF BABY BOOMER WOMEN
(WWW.NABBW.COM)

Danielle Bernock's memoir *"Emerging With Wings"* is a heart-felt, honest account of a journey through the injuries of life to a place of hope and healing. Her rich mix of spiritual passion, humor and vulnerability is bound to resonate with many readers.

KATHLEEN MCGUIRE-MOORE PH.D.
CLINICAL PSYCHOLOGIST

"Emerging With Wings" is a true story with which thousands will identify. The desire to be loved, protected and accepted. I thank God for a brave author who tells her story of seeking these very things and finds that she was not only loved, protected and accepted all along but was actually pursued by divine grace.

PASTOR KENT W. CLARK
CEO OF GRACE CENTERS OF HOPE

I have known Danielle Bernock for over 10 years and have witnessed the multiple changes she has experienced prior to, during, and after her journey of writing *"Emerging With Wings."* Dani divulges her most intimate and vulnerable moments in life and leads us on a journey using her own personal struggle to triumph. Her story added validation to multiple issues that I did not even know existed in my own life. With this came a realization that who she refers to as 'The Pursuer' was always there showing me His love and acceptance of me. I had not realized until after reading this book how issues that had been concealed had affected my thoughts toward multiple different people and situations in my life. This book has truly inspired me to open my eyes to other people's situations and consider how many hidden issues they may have as well. Although there is an ending to this book there is never an ending to 'The Pursuer' and what He can do in our lives.

CHRISTY MILIOTO
THE BFF
WORKING MOTHER

"Emerging With Wings" is the story of a real person sharing her journey with such a courageous vulnerability and openness that it helps others unravel their own story to find hope, healing and unconditional love. Everyone has their own version of lies and pain that has shaped their perception of themselves and their worth and reading Danielle Bernock's story helped bring to light many of the lies I had been believing in my own life. It opened my eyes to see ways in which what she calls 'The Pursuer' has been there for me all along telling me I am loved, I am valuable and I matter. Now I am grabbing ahold of that truth and getting my own wings.

STEPHANIE SANDERS
MOTHER TO SEVEN
FELLOW BELOVED OF THE PURSUER

Acknowledgments

The first person I would like to thank is you who are actually reading this page. In my research on how to write an acknowledgment page I found conflicting information. Some sources stressed how important it was and how I must include *everyone* while others would complain how trivial it was and that no one reads this section. So, thank YOU as you have made my investment of time worthwhile. You Matter!

The second person I would like to thank is the author Nelson Demille for his contribution on the Barnes and Noble *"The 25 Best Author Acknowledgments Ever Written."* I came across in my research mentioned above and found it both entertaining as well as helpful for me to not stress over my own. Thank you!

Next I would like to thank multiple engineers and scientists that have brought us the internet along with the plethora of contributors on the web who aided me in my research both in content as well as how to get this book from written to market. You taught me so very much from paper cuts and microsurgery to front matter and copyright. My appreciation is sincere. This book would not exist without you.

Thank you to all the people in my life that have been a positive influence on me. I cannot possibly list you all. However I must single out Joyce Meyer whose vulnerability and courage have given me the courage to be vulnerable in this book and to Sara Bareilles for her song *"Brave"* that helped me "let the words fall out."

I also need to thank the many people who listened to me talk about this project seemingly incessantly for the year and a half it took to complete the first edition. Your patience, support and encouragement did not go unnoticed. Your questions were quite helpful! And for this second edition a big thank you to all my readers for your feedback and to "my friend" (wink) for all your grammar help and encouragement. Thank you to all my endorsers for believing in me and supporting me.

A huge thank you to my counselor, Kathleen McGuire-Moore PhD. Your insight, questions and validation have changed my life. I am so thankful to have had your counsel through the writing process of this book. You escorted me to the much needed closure in my life. You then helped me pace myself while taking courage to both publish and promote my story to help others. I cannot thank you enough.

And my children, Naomi and Nathan I know you did not choose me as your mother but if I were given the opportunity to choose my children I would choose you all over again. It is a privilege to be your mother. We are not perfect. We have laughed and we have cried. I still choose you. You have changed my life repetitively in ways you cannot imagine. Thank you for the specific question I have included in this book from each of you as well as how you asked it. I love you with all my heart. May you always know You Matter!

My BFF, Christy Milioto, your support and loyal friendship is beyond words. I wouldn't be who I am without you. Thank you for encouraging me when I was frustrated, being one of my first readers, proofreader, critic and other set of eyes. Thank you for being vulnerable yourself and sharing how my story impacted you for the whole world to read in the endorsements.

And finally my Husband, Michael Bernock, OMG! In addition to what is already written in the pages of this book regarding you I thank you for being my other first reader, proofreader, critic, sounding board, encourager when I was frustrated as well as sponsor and producer. Words are inadequate to express my love and gratitude to you as well as **The Pursuer** who "paired" us.

A Note to Readers

In this book there are multiple QR codes that
look like the box you see here. A smart phone with a
QR reader is needed to access the information in it.
They take you to a place on the internet. This one takes
you to the explanation of what a QR code is. The web addresses for
them are found at the back of the book for those who do not have
a smart phone or simply wish to view on a computer screen. These
are placed within the text of the story to enhance your experience as
they elaborate on the content that is in the text.

This book began more as a sentimental journey but became a transforming power as I dared to bring to light, face, work through and
then reveal things that had been long hidden.

You are invited to embark on an inspirational journey of discovery.
We live in what we know and discovery opens new possibilities to
us, creates adventure. Let your imagination and emotion carry you
beyond the superficial into the reasons and causes of who you are.
Are you where you want to be? Are you what you want to be? Are
you content and at peace within yourself?

Everyone has challenges in life. Some have more and some have
less. Some are visible and some are invisible. The visible ones are

easier to address as they are clearly seen. It is the invisible ones that create the most damage as they frequently go untreated and subsequently "infect" us internally. Even if we try to hide them, scars have voices and secrets are not silent. These need to be resolved for us to truly be free. The simple "get over it", "just stop that" or "it isn't that bad" are insufficient. There needs to be validation and process to heal. But to have something validated one must bring it out into the light to be seen, so that it becomes visible. Many cringe at this because it is painful in a way that some refuse to acknowledge. Having medical surgery is validated because it is visible. Reaching into one's mind, will and emotions some might call navel gazing. I call it emotional surgery and the path to the victory of internal freedom. I faced fear and shame. Encouragement empowered me to not be ashamed but to be brave and share because that would give me the power to both overcome and to inspire others. I chose to listen to courage and so this book now exists. I wish you wings.

Danielle

You may contact me via email or follow me on twitter:

dbernock@emergingwithwings.com   twitter: @dbernock

You can find more information and book availability at:
www.emergingwithwings.com

Preface

⤳⤳

"Taking responsibility for being exactly where you are gives you the power to be exactly where you want to be."
Author unknown

"Life is lived forwards but understood backwards."
Soren Kierkegaard

Decisions. Don't underestimate their power. With them we can change direction and transform our lives. I made the decision to start this book. I sat down and just started. I had no idea the remarkable journey writing this would take me on.

There are numerous people that have played a part in my life. Some in positive ways, some in negative ways, and some, inflicting trauma. I take responsibility for where I am today. I cannot undo things that have happened. What is done is done. However today is a new day and I have the power to decide how I will proceed. I choose to learn and grow instead of blame. I hold no grudges. I let go of pain. I forgive. I have learned that people are people – they have problems and sometimes those problems crash into other people and cause harm. Sometimes there is malice and sometimes there is not. I recognize that what really happened in my life and what I perceived may not be exact. I have learned perception is reality to the one in the experience. I see now that I had choices I was not aware of. I had power I did not know how to operate. I made decisions on how to respond to whatever "they" did without understanding. This book looks back for the purpose of sharing the understanding I have gained. I choose to live my life going forward putting into effect the things I have come to understand as well as continue to learn.

I invite you into my story. I believe my story has been many things, but at this point in the story line I mainly see it as an amazing love story. The story of an invisible LOVE so huge and so pure it wills to never give up. This LOVE pursues a terrified and filthy child who does everything they can to hide and not be found. Why is this child so terrified and filthy? What is it about this child that this LOVE pursues it? The child is terrorized by a jealous abusive bully and his gang aka *the JAB!*. This LOVE is referred to as **The Pursuer** who is an amazing and real being aka God. The leader of *the JAB!* gang is the devil (or satan). The subordinates in the gang *(JAB!)* consist of his demons (fallen angels), the mistakes, weaknesses, failings and/or choices of others and my own ignorant negative mind. I am the child.

1

❧From Start to Apprehended❦

I don't remember when I first came in contact with **The Pursuer.** I went to a place called church to visit him when I was little. I remember that I loved this place. I loved the songs. I loved the crafts. I learned a song called *"How Great Thou Art"* that had so many verses and so many words on multiple poster boards that were set up on an easel while we sang. But what captivated me was the wonder of who that song was talking about. I wanted to know him. Who was he?

In grade school I came to see this person they talked about at church (God) as very complicated and very demanding. He was scary and I didn't really know what to do with that. I liked the God in that song. After I was all grown up, I came to know that **The Pursuer** (LOVE) was there back then. He was the God guy in the song. He was at work bringing information about Himself to that place called church through a thing called a pastor. I don't remember

21

this pastor guy because I was too little but I believe he would have taught us about the God in that song. I was told later that he knew something about that third person of what they called the Trinity. Like in the song, *"God in three persons, Blessed Trinity."* I didn't know what that meant but they defined it as the Father, Son and Holy Ghost. I heard of the Father. To me he was the big kahuna, head honcho, scary, the demanding one. Then there was Jesus. He was called the son of God. I was told he loved me, died, and rose again. Ok sure. So he was the complicated one. But this third guy called the Holy Ghost or Spirit or whatever, I didn't know anything else about him except that they add him on sorta like a footnote. However, this pastor guy didn't get to teach us anything at all. *The JAB!* intercepted him, stole this information and caused much harm to many people. He did it by getting this pastor guy voted out for the very reason I wish he would have stayed. Voted. Hmmm. I had no idea they did that stuff. I thought God was in charge of that kind of stuff. I thought that church place was His house.

Anyways, after they got rid of this pastor my dad wouldn't go to church because he didn't like the interim pastor, or the permanent one that followed. I don't know why he didn't like the interim one but he said the permanent one sounded like that cartoon mouse. My mom liked the interim pastor so I think she went until he was replaced by the permanent pastor. I don't remember what my two older brothers did. I do remember going with my mom one time to some other church to see the interim pastor after he had left our church. All I remember from that visit was that he used an overhead projector and talked about Greek words and stuff. I had no clue. I was too little. I don't even remember if we went more than once or not. But once again, looking back I see **The Pursuer** was there trying to reveal Himself to me.

I continued to go to that place called church even after the new pastor arrived. I took the bus. It picked me up at the end of my street. Somehow I still loved going even though I went all by myself. I was perhaps nine at the time. I still remember the little jingle about what time it started – nine thirty sharp! That's until *the JAB!* got involved again. He crafted an evil plan that succeeded in getting me out of there. But he didn't even stop there. He was so mean and abusive to me, a real bully. Who he is and how he succeeded is part of my story. Back then I didn't even know he existed and a person doesn't fight something that isn't there. But, he was there and mangled my tender young soul quite invisibly. However, **The Pursuer** is passionate and refused to just let him have me. I just didn't know that at the time either. Lies well placed by *the JAB!* built a fortress of darkness in me. There were very many lies that I believed. I came to believe that the God guy didn't care, had abandoned me and cast me out as refuse. I knew nothing of **The Pursuer.**

Lies, Lies, Lies, and Trauma Building the Darkness

ℰ⒭

As a child I grew up wrestling with feelings and thoughts that I was adopted and didn't belong in my family. Why would I think such a thing? I did not know, I just felt disconnected or added as a footnote but not really wanted.

Now I know it was "simply" one part of the elaborate con *the JAB!* had pulled on me. And as I said, I didn't know he was there so I never challenged any of his stories. Lie validating stories like a poem my mother had written before I was born about her sons where she simply added my name in afterward, like a footnote *(JAB!)*.

Another was being told the neighbor boy was adopted along with the instructions to keep it a secret. If it was such a secret why were they telling me? And yet another when I found out I was not a planned pregnancy. My mother used the words "an accident" *(JAB!)* that pierced my heart like a sword. I don't know how old I was when I found this out but whenever it was, *the JAB!* made sure it left a deep wound validating his previous lie - I did not belong. This I translated in my soul to: Mistake, Not wanted, Tolerated, Without value... A well placed lie he built into a large edifice. So large it became that I arrived at the place of trying to invisibly kill myself as slowly as possible. But I am getting ahead of myself.

(Kindergarten – age 5)

My family was still going to church when I was in Kindergarten and I loved singing. I remember singing *"Away in the Manger"* in class for our Christmas party. My mom didn't like one of the verses and didn't want me to sing it. The one where Jesus takes us to heaven to live with him. But I especially liked that one. Because He *wanted* me with Him. I wasn't a footnote. He loved me. I loved this Jesus. Why wouldn't I want to be with him? Why didn't my mom want me to be with him? *(JAB!)* It confused me and made me afraid. Thinking back I imagine that it made her think of death, me dying and didn't want me to leave because she loved me. But I was five, what did I know? And back then you didn't talk to your parents about anything. I was told repeatedly that children were to be seen and not heard. So I never inquired. So the lie that the God "who loved me" might be dangerous was laid.

(1st grade – age 6)

First grade left a large scar. I remember my teacher's name, her being pregnant and being very mean. She went on maternity leave sometime during the year but not before being used by *the JAB!* to harm me. One day she gave instruction for us to be quiet – no talking. Sounds like a normal thing for a teacher to do, especially if our class was being unruly or something. But I was only 6 and therefore remember only pieces. Have you ever heard the line "punishment that fits the crime"? This teacher apparently did not. I was unfortunate enough to drop my pencil on the floor. I could not reach it. So I committed the heinous crime of talking! I asked the kid near my pencil if he would get it for me. He did. Well the teacher heard me speak and the punishment began. This 6 year old was initially sent out into the hall. I remember that being terrifying enough, but it got worse. I don't remember how long I was out there but I was brought back into the room for reading groups. The teacher subsequently put tape over my mouth and forced me to read in my group out loud with the tape over my mouth. The humiliation and shame was unbearable. I told no one. *The JAB!* used this to traumatize me and embed in my soul (well into adulthood) a fear to speak and be heard as well as the expectation that what I need is not important. He laid that lie nicely on top of the lie from Kindergarten. They fit together so well, like puzzle pieces. But they were still lies.

(grade school)

A good con man is a successful liar and must sell his lie as if it were the truth. *The JAB!* does this so well. He takes what is inherently truth and twists it just enough so it's close but it ceases to be true. He does this cleverly and repeatedly. **The Pursuer** knows this. He calls the head of *the JAB!* the Father of Lies. Another of his clever lies he sold to me was planted in a movie. I wish I knew the name of this movie or anything about it. I don't even know if I remember the movie correctly. I was just a small child. But I remember two things. I remember the moment of the violent piercing of my soul, like you see in the movies where the assailant stabs, twists the knife and gleefully watches as their victim falls incapacitated. I remember that I paid full price for the lie. I bought it – hook, line and sinker. In the movie some kid was talking to another kid about who knows what. One of them quoted from Matthew 10 in the Bible where it says: *"Are not two sparrows sold for a farthing? And one of them shall not fall on the ground without your Father. But the very hairs of your head are all numbered. Fear ye not therefore; ye are of more value than many sparrows. The JAB!* whissspered… *"Does God care? Really? He let that sparrow fall. He doesn't care. Not about that sparrow or you. You are of no value at all!"* How vile a lie and so similar to his first. The one in the garden he sold to Eve. Questioning LOVE. Striking at the very heart of **The Pursuer** who IS LOVE and therefore does LOVE. *The JAB!* knew the truth. Yes, he knew the truth and that is what made him so out of his mind mad and so vicious. He was jealous. He hated me and he hated **The Pursuer.** He hated all **The Pursuer** had created. He wanted it for himself. He knew that **The Pursuer** considered me of supreme value, greatly prized – just like that Bible verse says "more value." The "more value" is that I am worth the very life blood of his son. But I didn't see that back then. I saw the lie. I believed the lie. I did not grasp the truth of **The Pursuer's** love for me until the year I am writing this book. Lies are vile. Believing them is harmful at best, deadly at worst.

(grade school – Music)

My dad had a beautiful bass voice. My mother played

piano. There was a lady from that church place that played violin. They would get together to play and sing. I loved my dad's voice when he sang. **The Pursuer** had given me a love for music and singing. He used it as often as possible to Bless me. I played violin. I played piano. I was pretty good too for being in grade school. Not a prodigy mind you at all – just pleasantly adequate. However this apparently angered *the JAB!* because he got his lies in there too. I had a concert pianist as an instructor. She was tough but she was excellent. My first recital piece I played flawlessly. However, while I was practicing the piano like any other day I had a difficult time with a particular piece. I kept making mistakes. Because of this, I am instructed by my mother that I must practice this same piece over and over until I can play it without one mistake. I believe my mom simply wanted me to succeed but *the JAB!* whispered *"nothing short of perfection is good enough."* Each time I began the song fear grew and each time I made another mistake. I got worse instead of better. Over and over and over, until it felt like forever. I never did get it perfect. Fear won and I failed. Another lie, *"Never good enough"* was successfully sold.

The next blow was after spending months perfecting a different piece for the next recital. This piece was quite difficult but I learned to play it flawlessly as I did the first one. However a conflict of schedules arose. The date of the recital and the date of a family friend's wedding were the same. I could not go to both. The decision was made to attend the wedding instead of the recital. When I arrived at my next lesson we were informed she would no longer have me as a student. *The JAB!* whispers again *"unwanted, not good enough."* I believe she might have stated the ultimatum on the front end or even if she didn't, I can see how my absence at the recital may have done her harm *(JAB!)*. He attacked us both. I did get another teacher but it was never the same. The passion was gone *(JAB!)*. He successfully stole that.

Next in line was my singing. I can just see them laughing and rubbing their hands together in glee anticipating the next scheme. I was in the chorus in sixth grade and was chosen for a solo. I was a soprano at the time. We were to perform two times: once in a school assembly and once in an evening performance. For reasons I do not know I forgot every single word of my solo while standing in front of the entire school. Really?? I had sung in front of people before. What happened?? *The JAB!* whispers *"idiot, not good enough"* which is only accentuated with my classmates laughing and pointing and teasing me upon returning to the classroom. I tell my music teacher I will not be singing at the evening performance. I simply couldn't bear doing it again. The shame and humiliation were unbearable. But arguing with adults was not something done so I complied and agreed to sing that night. I was successful at singing it, even though the mother, yes, the mother, of one of my classmates sat on the front row laughing and pointing at me *(JAB!)*. That drove my singing passion inward. I moved to the alto section in chorus in an attempt to hide and belong. My voice successfully silenced, I never took singing in junior high or high school. In fact, for fear of ridicule and *"not belonging"* in junior high I even dropped the violin after sixth grade. Another score for *the JAB!*.

(grade school – 5th ? *"conversion"*)

Also in grade school after my parents had stopped going to church *the JAB!* plotted to get me out of that church place. As I said, I continued to go after they stopped. I rode the bus. One particular Sunday **The Pursuer** was inviting me to receive his love gift Jesus. I was in the big people service that day and I to this day do not remember why. I imagine **The Pursuer** orchestrated it somehow because He is LOVE and wants me, as well as everyone else, to know it. I usually just went to Sunday School with the kids. I was perhaps ten maybe eleven years old. I didn't know that was what was happening at the time but I still remember the pulling like a magnet to respond. The pastor did what they call an altar call that day. I don't know if I even knew what one of those was at the time. The way I remember the altar call was that the pastor asked us if we knew there was something wrong between us and God. I didn't even know what he meant by that, but I somehow knew it applied to me and it scared me. But still I felt that magnetic like pull. They played the hymn *"Just As I Am"* over and over as they waited for someone to respond. After what felt like a million times, I could stand it no longer. I got up from my seat, which was in the back of the sanctuary, and walked to the front where the pastor stood. The walk felt like miles long. I felt like everyone was glaring at me. When I finally arrived at the front with the pastor, he greeted me with "thank you." That confused me. I was coming forward for the answer to the question he had asked yet felt like he was thanking me for responding when no one else did. Like I bailed him out of looking bad or something *(JAB!)*. He then proceeded to send me off with some lady I didn't know *(JAB!)* who took me to a room and asked me what was wrong *(JAB!)*. I didn't know – I thought the pastor was going to tell me that. I loved my pastor – who was this lady?? I don't remember anything else from my encounter with her. It's almost like *the JAB!* knocked me senseless with *"You don't matter" "I don't have time for you" "How could you be so stupid?" "Why are you wasting our time?" "What is wrong with you anyways?"*... What I do remember is that I started membership classes and subsequently was baptized confessing Jesus as my personal savior. So in there somewhere, somehow, **The Pursuer** was able to deliver his love gift of Jesus to me, even if in a small way and even though *the JAB!* had successfully wounded me. Remember, I still didn't know *the JAB!* was even there so I internalized all the blame. That's what children do.

(6th?? grade Baptism)

It was springtime on the day I got baptized. I believe my family came to church also. I find it interesting that I have to say *"I believe,"* because I don't remember. Other than remembering actually **being** baptized, the way that I remember anything else of that day is only due to an internal snapshot of me and my mom. I remember that she and I were in the back, behind the stage somewhere and next to stairs. I was wearing a pale yellow shirt dress. Back then girls were required to wear dresses to church and school. I had a Bible I had received as a gift for my baptism. I don't remember my dad or brothers being there but I imagine that they must have been. I think we might have gone out to eat too, but again I am not sure. Why all this lack of memory? I find it disturbing. Perhaps it was the wounding that occurred. I cannot say for certain. But the wounding was nothing in comparison with what was to come.

(6th grade?? Church humiliation)

Sometime after this was the Sunday where they would recognize me and welcome me as a new member. I rode the bus that day and was so excited. I was going to be accepted. I was going to belong. They sat all of us who had been baptized and completed the membership class as a group. We were on display in the front row on the right side of the church. I believe all of us were children. One by one the names were called to summon us to the front. However, my name was never called *(JAB!)*. They left me sitting on that front row all by myself on display for the whole church to see my exclusion *(JAB!)*. I was given no explanation. I was given no comfort. I cried all the way home on the bus, alone. *The JAB!* whissspering *"see, I told you that God guy didn't care about you! You don't belong anywhere! NO one wants you!"* I was beyond devastated – now, I was impaired. *The JAB!* had successfully and invisibly delivered a bull's-eye lie as well as led me to believe I must strive to earn to be accepted, to have any place at all. So that is what I proceeded to do. I came to learn that they had refused me membership because my parents who were members stopped attending. They said if they made me a member I would just stop coming also. But they said that if I proved myself that they would change their decision. So I did. I went every Sunday until they accepted me. Earning acceptance is a lie *the JAB!* crafted to keep people from **The Pursuer.** In truth the love and grace of **The Pursuer** is freely available to all. But they offered no grace. After I worked my way into their "graces" even that was substandard. They agreed to make me a member but did it on a Sunday night in a hidden kind of way. And *the JAB!* whispers *"see! your value is insufficient for display before all."* It is a sad thing that the church people became self-proclaiming prophets – that was the last time I remember going. I stopped, just like my parents. *The JAB!* attacked them too.

(6th grade school humiliation, age – 11)

At this same time *the JAB!* pulled off more of his plan in my social life also. He had infiltrated my home life, my school life, my church life and now he was after the friend circle. It was October,

I was in the sixth grade and the kids that were allowed to were out doing their pranks. (We were not allowed.) Back then soaping or waxing windows and ringing door bells were the biggies I remember. A kid came by and put either soap or wax on the back window of my mom's station wagon that was parked in the driveway. One of my brothers ran to apprehend him. Without going into detail, the chase got ugly and ended in a nasty way. *The JAB!* took full advantage of the situation and turned the nasty back onto me. I arrived at school the next time greeted by my entire class as a threatening mob. And *the JAB!* whispered *"now you'll NEVER belong."* How I survived sixth grade must have simply been because **The Pursuer** carried me. He loved me and He did this even though I didn't recognize him or know how to reach out for help.

(grade school / junior high – Bible mangled)

Somewhere in that time line between receiving Jesus and leaving the church I was instructed that if I didn't read my Bible every day that it was a sin. Another *"no grace"* thing they put in me. So, like a nice compliant little girl I obeyed. I didn't know it then, but fear is the language of *the JAB!* And I obeyed because I was afraid *(JAB!)*. I would open my Bible to just anywhere and read – just so I wasn't sinning *(JAB!)*. This is **not** how **The Pursuer** desires us to learn of Him. LOVE had given the Bible aka The WORD as a gift to reveal Himself to us, not beat us over the head. That third person called the Holy Spirit was intended to guide us gracefully through His LOVE story. But, I did not learn that until very many years later. Consequently *the JAB!* was successful at causing me to read things out of context and with a negative perception which caused torment. That is what fear does, it torments. However, **The Pursuer** loved me, and being the LOVE gentleman that He is, found a way back in. Someone gave me a little book that contained the book of Psalms separate from the entire Bible. That brought me comfort and hope. But I still kept reading my Bible randomly out of fear, wanting that God guy to accept me or at least not throw me away like I feared. So the two battled inside me.

THE BULLIES

ഇൗരു

Not wanting to lose the battle to **The Pursuer** *the JAB!* sent some bullies with skin on. Two of them were effective at torment but the third changed my life forever. One of the bullies was a boy I was hopelessly infatuated with. Looking back I cannot understand why. It simply must have been *the JAB!*. I cried over this boy and played sad songs to myself about this boy only for him to call me Pig instead of my name and think that it was hilarious. For two years I lived with him calling me that. Every time he said it *the JAB!* would whisper *"worthless."* The second one was another boy that at the beginning I was told liked me but I wasn't interested in him. But we became friends. Or so I thought. Then the betrayal. He became friends with bully #1 and joined in the name calling with him. Now *the JAB!* had his whisper of *"worthless"* in stereo. As painful as that was and tedious as what we call Chinese water torture, it doesn't compare to bully #3.

Bully #3 was a girl. She was what was understood as "the coolest person in school." You know the kind. Everyone listens to them. They carry such weight even though you don't know why. She was related to my next door neighbor. I was friends with my next door neighbor's younger sister. That alone brought me ridicule because I "didn't play with people my own age." But those "people my own age" were not accessible to me. I had been separated

33

from them by something I didn't understand. It was a curse wall *the JAB!* put in place. I believed all his lies and now they played out in my life. I felt I didn't belong and so I didn't. Anyways, bully #3 played a very large role in my life. She used to call me "dog" all the time degrading not only me but my family as a whole. You see, my parents got quite invested in their hobby of dogs after leaving the church. They bred Labrador Retrievers for show and field trialing. It pretty much ran our life whether we liked it or not. Every day or so we would have to go out somewhere to train with the dogs after dinner as well as on weekends and all vacations. They were clearly the priority. We went many places to attend field trials and went to the dog shows. So I got around a lot – but it was clear to me that the travel was for the dogs and I was just along for the ride. So this derogatory nickname was a dig every time I heard it. It said *"haha – you know she's right – you are second rate, they didn't want you in the first place."* She was a constant voice of *the JAB!* every time I had contact with her until the life changing incident. I don't know when it was and remember very little after it due to the magnitude of the trauma it inflicted to my soul.

As I stated earlier I had issue with belonging in my family. I believed the lies of *the JAB!* that I was not wanted. He hammered that in every chance he got. Back then I carried a different name than I do now. The name I was given at birth was Diane. Well, one day, for reasons I do not know, Bully #3 was chasing me. She started chasing me around and around a car that was parked in the street in front of my neighbor's house and she was screaming at me. She screamed with the voice of *the JAB!* with a blow to my soul that words cannot convey with accuracy. The soul damage far exceeded the piercing from the movie I told you about. She screamed "Do you know WHY your parents named you Diane???? Do you know why??? They didn't want you!! They named you Diane so that *EVERY TIME THEY SAY YOUR NAME* they are saying *DIE ANN! DIE Ann! Die Ann! Die Ann!..." the JAB!* echoing the whisper in the background saying *"you don't deserve to exist, worthless, just die."* I told no one. I had no voice. I believed she was right. How I didn't go home and commit suicide after that I must give credit to **The Pursuer.** Somehow, someway he kept me alive so he could make a way to rescue me from my invisible cage. He even brought people into my life who would counter those words by stating what a lovely name I had but I was deaf to that. I despised the name and I secretly despised myself.

DEATH, DEATH, DEATH!

☠ ☠ ☠

I had a very small family. My mom was an only child and had lost her dad back when she was little. My grandma had remarried but it was not very ideal. My mom was around twelve when her mom remarried a widower with grown children. He was an old school overbearing Greek man. It not being his first marriage he let my grandmother know that he had raised his kids and he wasn't about to do it again. This meant my mom had to make her own way. My mom got a job as soon as she was old enough. (I now see *the JAB!* was busy here also.) I pretty much had no relationship with my grandpa even though he was the only grandpa I ever knew. But my grandma – I loved her dearly. She was a very old school German immigrant who always wore dresses, had beautiful silver hair and was a master gardener. I would stay at her house when my mom and dad went on vacation until I got old enough to go to camp. Every memory I have of my grandma is wonderful. I can still visit her house in my mind. I remember every room. Even now it makes my heart smile to think of my memories of her. Like when she was watching my brother's finches for them while they were at camp and one flew away while she was cleaning the cage. She saw where it flew into a neighbor's tree. She sat beneath that tree in a folding chair and learned how to whistle that day. She sat there all day until that bird actually came back! My dad's family had all died except for a brother when I came along. My mom had met his dad but he died before they were even married. My dad's brother was a part of our lives at the beginning of my growing up but then suddenly was not, for reasons I never knew. Sounds like *the JAB!* was busy here too.

(junior high)

In the summer of 1972 *the JAB!* was at it again. My grandmother suffered a heart attack. I was devastated. I actually prayed to that God guy or Jesus or something. I pleaded with him for her life because of all these great reasons, one being that I needed her. I was hoping the lies were not true, that I mattered and that He would save her – for me. And if not for me then at least for the girl down the street my grandma knew that had just suffered a terrible motorcycle accident. But she died only days later on July 25th and *the JAB!* whispered *"see he doesn't care, he killed your grandma, he doesn't listen to you, you can't trust him, he doesn't care what you need...."* I accused God. I started to sink only for the waters to rise even higher. On Friday September 22nd the same year, *the JAB!* viciously stole my Dad. He had a heart attack right in front of me and my mother with all the horrid noises that go with it. It was loud and terrifying. My mother, who to me had always been such a controlled rational stable person, became hysterical before my eyes. She screamed for me to call 911 only to grab the phone from me to complete the conversation. By the time the paramedics arrived he was already dead but they took him to the hospital anyways – DOA. Both my brothers were not home but arrived during the crisis. This became like unto an atomic bomb in our family. *The JAB!* having successfully separated us from church and family to help – we imploded. I barely remember that there was a funeral at all. My mother lost her mom and her husband within two months of each other, making her injured for us her kids who suffered the losses on different levels. We all got self-involved as well as involved in unhealthy crutches. I sank into self-pity, sad depressing songs, alcohol and then drugs to numb pain.

Not quite four years later...

I successfully graduated from high school. Strange that I could do so well being so withdrawn and angst-ridden. I was in the Honor Society and didn't even understand what it was or how I got in it. I went to cosmetology school as a junior and senior through a co-op program at school. I think I did it just to get out of going to school half the day every day. But I finished it and got my license anyways. Most of it is a blur with moments of clarity. Looking back I see these "moments of clarity" were most likely **The Pursuer** inserting hope into my life. I am amazed as I look back and see the plethora of such insertions. Before I started looking back for good things, all I saw and remembered was the bad. Perhaps that is something that adds to my amazement. This LOVE, this **Pursuer** is amazing! I remember that due to our financial situation I got 'free lunches,' which I sold for less than the cost of the lunch so that I could buy a chocolate shake and a bag of a new kind of chips I especially liked! I remember the two lunches that everyone wanted my lunch ticket for: Baked Italian Noodles and Pizza Burgers! The Baked Italian

Noodles always came with fresh homemade cinnamon buns. Those were worth a lot to the kids as they were perhaps the best thing that ever came out of the kitchen and they'd run out of them quickly. Ha! Silly things to remember. I remember taking all the sewing classes the school offered leading to gaining a special class called Independent Study in my senior year. A class they allowed only if permission is acquired and a sponsoring teacher is secured. I not only acquired permission but secured an unusual sponsoring teacher. The teacher that sponsored me was a woman that had disliked me and had it in for me when we first met. We had become friends. Points for **The Pursuer**! I remember being on the gymnastics team. I remember when competing on the uneven parallel bars I would not hear a sound. I remember that humungous trampoline with the harness to learn flips – oh what fun. Those two things have long gone away. The uneven bars of that time do not resemble what they use now. And so far as I know, due to liability issues, trampolines are non-existent in schools now. I'm glad I remember them. These little memories that are like tiny rays of light shining into a dark hole. Each tiny ray seemingly insignificant yet when gathered all together they resemble looking at the stars.

Ever since I was ten years old I went to camp every summer. It was a bright ray of light in my life. Upon graduation I did the same thing. Only this time I was a counselor. Looking back I think to myself – *really? Seriously? You were a mess!!* But things were about to get even worse. I was up at camp and suddenly I saw my mother driving in and she had her best friend with her. *Hmm smells like trouble.* So I rationalized that my step grandfather must have died because he had been having health issues. *Yup, that must be it.* I thought to myself. However – I was not correct. Funny things these things called our minds. We think it and therefore we decide it's true. What that is really called is self-deception *(JAB!)*. Self-deception is never good. Truth always comes to light. And so it did here as well. I was summoned to the counselor's cabin so my mother could speak with me. For some reason she took me outside and over to the side of the cabin for the conversation. She proceeded to inform me that David, my eldest brother, who I loved more than life, was dead and had been murdered *(JAB!)*. I remember two things. I screamed and I passed out. I woke up inside the counselor's cabin lying down somewhere. They gave me a tranquilizer and took me home. I remember I was gone a week but I could not tell you what I did during that week. I do remember (whether it was before I went home or after I returned I don't know) telling my boyfriend (who worked at the camp also) about my brother. Murdered! I was beyond mad. I didn't know it when it happened, but that was when 'hate' attached itself to me. That was the beginning of a new spiral downward. Unless I look at photographs, the only other thing I remember of that summer was my mother driving up to camp on my 18th birthday to give me my first legal drink in the parking lot. My mother and I had many issues back then but at least she was still around for me. It was another ray of light.

I felt so dirty, so unlovable. Why were all these people leaving me? As if their dying was of their own intention to leave me. More of that self-deception *(JAB!)*. And I blamed that God guy I had heard about when I was "little" *(JAB!)*. I reasoned that if He really loved me that all this bad stuff would never have happened. More self-deception *(JAB!)*. And so I went through the summer burying my emotions in getting high and transferring the excess devotion I had to my brother David onto my boyfriend, who conveniently proposed to me. However when the summer ended I went home, and so did my "fiancé." He still had one more year of high school to finish before we could get married, AND his family had moved to Minnesota. I spent the next few months working and severely dieting to lose the weight I gained over the summer so I would be skinny for this announcement. But instead of "happily ever after" like the fantasy in my head, I got more devastation *(JAB!)*. The plan had been that my fiancé would come to Michigan at Christmas and we would announce our engagement. However instead of this lovely (cue romantic music) illusion…. I receive a letter on Christmas Eve *(JAB!)*. A "dear John" letter that says "we were like two fish swimming through the sea bowl of life…" Really? *(JAB!)* Really. I don't remember anything else specific of the letter. It was so appalling it left a mark. I remember my brother Tim in an act of love for me, called him to confront him, although I confess I remember nothing of the conversation. I don't remember that Christmas at all either. It is quite possible I spent it wasted under the influence of whatever I could get my hands on to rid me of the pain of wanting to fall down dead *(JAB!)*. I felt like refuse tossed into a garbage heap with no hope of recovery. I felt stripped of everything of value even though that was not true. What I felt ruled my life *(JAB!)*. Loss, loss, loss, loss. Would it ever end??? I wondered. It must be my fault I thought *(JAB!)*. This is when what little self-respect I had retained departed my life. The dieting turned into eating disorders as I began surviving on thirty to a hundred calories a day only to shift into bulimia (the bingeing and purging). I found the bulimia much more malicious and self-debasing – which was my goal *(JAB!)*. Pain and I were friends. Pain was how I felt anything. How I lived past this is purely the protection of **The Pursuer.** I kept bad company *(JAB!)*. I put myself in harm's way more than I would even be able to remember – physically, emotionally, sexually and spiritually *(JAB!)*. Smoking, parties with drugs, drunk driving and alcohol black outs, drugs of various kinds (one time I was given the wrong stuff), bulimia, sex, adultery, various occult practices, new age religion… I was so hurt. I was so mad. I could only take it out on myself *(JAB!)*. Inwardly convulsing, I was so lost.

I had another one of those self-deception thoughts that I held close like a teddy bear. My brother David had gone out to California sometime before he died and somehow I believed my solution was to do the same. So my quest to go to California began. I had one trip planned with a girlfriend but it fell through. She wasn't known for being reliable so I wasn't devastated, just resolute to find another way. My next attempt was putting an ad in the paper for someone to go with because so far I was still attached to the idea that I needed someone to go with me. Well that turned into something you might expect to see on TV. I had one female respond so I set up a meet with her to see if it would work. We met at some little place down in the rich part of town where one might feel safer. In the course of our consultation it became necessary to call 911 for her as she was mentally unstable. Details escape me. Again I am amazed at the protection **The Pursuer** exercised here. It was after this situation that I started to contemplate going to California alone. Somehow I believed I "needed" to go. As I was contemplating this, I was also a student at the community college close to home. I was in the girls lavatory lounge smoking between classes and a fellow student came in. She said something that changed my life. She said "Do you know anyone who wants to go to California?" I immediately responded that I did. She didn't believe me and said she was serious. I told her she had no idea just how serious I was. And so plans were made. **The Pursuer** provided for me.

CALIFORNIA ROAD TRIP

❧❧❧❧

Cheryl and I departed on our road trip to California on May 16 at 7:30 a.m. in my 1973 Pontiac LeMans I called Babe. That was way back when there was no such thing as a cell phone. There were just land line house phones and people paid extra for long distance and a thing called person to person calls, etc. So because we were girls it was decided "for our safety" that we were to call our parents every day alternating days with each other. We were to call collect and ask for ourselves by name thereby letting our parents know that we were safe. If they wanted to talk to us they would have to say they were us and accept the charges. Texting nowadays is so much easier! And so we were off on our adventure. For reasons I do not know (perhaps she told me but I don't remember) she brought her Bible with her. She had something called a Good News Bible. I had never heard of it. And for reasons I do not know I brought my Bible also. My guess is it had something to do with that acceptance and belonging I wanted so badly. I had that old King James Bible from back when I got baptized. That thing I avoided now because either it made no sense at all or it condemned me *(JAB!)*. At any rate, I brought it and we read to each other while we drove. We read while we got high but we read, and we drove and we read and we drove and we read. I had no idea that with that we were inviting **The Pursuer** to come with us, and come with us He did.

Soon another alteration in the direction of my life occurred. I actually prayed. Couldn't tell you when I had last done that. The situation was that we were in Colorado stopped to make our daily person to person collect call. The operator told me about the weather situation. That was strange because you didn't carry on conversations with the operator but **The Pursuer** had been invited and here He was to protect us. A tornado was in the area *(JAB!)*. I was scared so I prayed and asked God to keep us safe. And to my shock and amazement Cheryl and I both saw a sign in the sky. The clouds moved in a way that looked to be out stretched arms covering us. Some might not believe me but I can say that it was real to me and **The Pursuer** answered me and kept us safe. Of course I had no idea it was **The Pursuer.** To me it was that God guy who I had been mad at because I blamed him for everything. So I thought this was out of character for him. Especially because I had been trying to prove he didn't exist because I had gathered enough lies to believe that if he did exist I was in more trouble than I could comprehend. But his character is actually quite different from the perception I had at the time. Even though I was puzzled I was grateful so I thanked him. So, on we went. We drove, read the Bible and partied. I kept a journal on my trip and find it interesting the amount of times I say that "I'm thankful" or "thank God," evidence that reading the Bible is affecting me. One amusing entry is "I just hope God stays with us to keep us safe. I know he will if we deserve it. I feel we've been doing right." Really?? – doing right (roll eyes). Right there is evidence of my incorrect perception *(JAB!)* of **The Pursuer's** heart and his Son Jesus. I think I have to earn his love and protection. I do not. As will be evidenced in a little bit here where **The Pursuer's** love and protection for us is obvious in the face of utter stupidity.

From Colorado we went to Las Vegas. Not a favorite place for various reasons. One being before leaving we needed to replace the shocks in Babe. So while that was getting done Cheryl went to shoot pool with the gas station owner who put something in her drink *(JAB!)*. Another place for thankfulness as we got out of there in one piece and we made it to San Diego just before Memorial Day.

San Diego was our favorite place. Beautiful campground, nice people, new friends, the best zoo, sunshine... sunburn, ouch! We arrived on Thursday. Sunday Cheryl went to church, I stayed at the campsite and read Genesis. Tuesday we went to Blacks Beach (clothing optional). While at the Beach, Babe breaks again. We were parked on a hill and Babe was leaking gasoline all down the hill. Having no idea what to do due to being in a strange place, we were happy three marines came to our rescue. One drove us all over to get the situation taken care of – new fuel pump. Afterward two of them hung out and got high with us. Then Cheryl and I went to Pacific Beach before going back to the campground to party with new friends there. Our two marines joined us back at the campground. They became our companions for a few days. We went to a couple of amusement parks and Malibu Beach together before heading our separate ways. In all this **The Pursuer** is still... pursuing me. I bought a teeny tiny cross for myself at one of the amusement parks. Hmmm **The Pursuer** is starting to leave fingerprints.

Heading up to Oregon I get pulled over in a rather odd way. One of two times. This policeman has me follow him while he pulls the car over that was following me. After he gives that white car a ticket he comes to my car. While he's talking to me someone runs up to him, says something, then he tells me to forget it and just move on. Ticket averted – I thank God even using the word "lord." Hmmm more fingerprints. Right after this Babe breaks AGAIN. We got stuck in Fresno until six p.m. getting a new distributor so we decided to drive all night to Lake Tahoe. We get to see some big redwoods but we are bumming out that we missed out on Yosemite and wonder if we will have to skip Washington, Oregon, Idaho, Montana.... money problems. After spending the day at

Pope Beach we head to our campsite and get pretty wasted with some new friends. We spent another day at Pope's Beach where we met more guys, went to their place, partied and enjoyed a sauna and Jacuzzi. We slept there and our tent slept alone. Not a brilliant move, yet **The Pursuer** protected us once again. We are unaware of our foolishness and his protection, but that is about to change.

Thursday morning we left for Pendleton Oregon deciding to go a different way than previously planned. We drove all day, night and into the morning. We partied while we drove. Fifteen and a half hours we drove. When we arrived it was two thirty in the morning and I got pulled over – bummer! But wait, here is that part in the story where **The Pursuer** intervenes causing one to say "are you serious??" So here I am: exhausted from driving, wasted from getting high and drinking, upset from having hit a rabbit with my car, having missed a deer, two raccoons, an opossum and a squirrel, lost AND driving the wrong way on a one way road!! Did you say it? Think it? "Are you serious???" Yes, I am and have it documented in my journal or I wouldn't remember it or believe it either. But wait there is still more (I know, sounds like an infomercial). The policeman that stops me, is friendly, escorts me to a park where I can park my car and we can sleep in it AND only writes me a warning! Can you say amazed?! **The Pursuer** got my attention here even though I am quite screwed in the head. I wrote a song about going the wrong way on a one way road and included spiritual implications.

So we did make it to Oregon (got my coveted wool blanket), Washington, Idaho (loved the trees) and Montana. While in Montana Cheryl did her check in phone call and our financial situation is revealed. No one is happy. Earlier in the trip we would skip eating to lose weight, now we are not eating to save money too.

45

The Pursuer has impressed me so much that at least I have hope. I am hoping "he stays up there looking in on us."

So we are off to Yellowstone, in the rain. The place was a disappointment as it was cold and wet. We pitched our tent and went looking for a fire nearby but came away empty. Went to bed with some bourbon to be warm and awoke to two inches of snow just beginning to seep into the tent. Happy June. Went to see the famous geyser but could not due to snow but they did have a cafeteria where we were able to get some hot food. Then we headed east and things got prettier – mountains, trees, colors…

On our way to Black Hills Deadwood South Dakota Babe broke AGAIN. I *(JAB!)* ran her a hundred miles per hour with loose and worn belts and she broke one (power steering) and stretched the other one (alternator). She overheated badly and we spent the night in Greybull Wyoming. I called my mom – twice. I was so upset and she really helped. She had gone "back to church" herself sometime before my road trip began. It was a different church than before and she had a group of friends praying for Cheryl and I. Mom was known for being calm in crisis situations and being solution minded – two skills I did not possess. As I said earlier, whatever I felt is what was in control and made me quite a powerless person. True to form she came to the rescue with a wire transfer in addition to emotional help. We got Babe fixed for fifteen dollars and we were mobile again. We headed to Mt Rushmore and stopped at a park before Babe stalled again while we were smoking a bowl. Finally got her started again discovering the issue to be bad gas + altitude = problems.

We found the Badlands to be gorgeous. We laid in the sun, got some oil for Babe and true to form met more people to party with. But out of the norm, the topic of the evening's discussion was God, different names for him and such. As strange and incorrect as some of the information was – **The Pursuer** found a way to at least bring attention to himself. For four hours we talked. One guy, Bill, had some pretty strange beliefs, like the world was gonna end in 1992 which obviously didn't happen. But he knew some stuff that was in the Bible too. Stuff about Israel, about some ten headed monster, three corner something-or-other. I didn't understand but I was liking talking about this God guy again. I wrote in my journal that I felt I might know what I "conceive him to be" and then went all bizarre in my explanation by combining all the information from the various spiritual things I had gotten into (new age, occult, science, psychology…) but ended with "God I love you!" in response to all the beauty of his creation. I wrote: "GOD I AM SO HAPPY RIGHT NOW. I think I should be a research biologist." Declared as if it was the answer to all of the questions humanity had. Makes sense right? Everyone who is happy and appreciates nature should become a research biologist! I hope you laughed because that cracks me up. The sheer ridiculousness is humorous.

On the heels of that we head back to Michigan via the Upper Peninsula. We read a lot of the Good News Bible as we drove. I liked it, it made me feel light. But as we drove it began to rain, rain, rain, thunder, lightning, thunder, lightning… had to stop due to the weather. The lightning helped us to see, but it was raining just too hard, so we had to stop – at a rest area between Wisconsin and Minnesota. We'll just sleep in the car.

2

APPREHENDED to Michael

↖ ↗ ↙ ↘↖ ↗↙ ↘↖ ↗↙ ↘↖ ↗↙ ↘

Friday June 16th 1978 I woke up in the front seat of my car in the rest area between Minnesota and Wisconsin and something was different… I knew I was not alone. Although I did not see anyone beside Cheryl (who was asleep in the back seat), I knew someone else was there. I knew it. I felt it. It was a drawing, a pulling, like that magnetic force I felt before… also a yearning, a desire…. a voice without words loving me and I need to respond… to what I determined was that God guy. But then *(JAB!)* fear! I'd been trying to prove He didn't exist. He must be mad… fear *(JAB!)* a demanding, an ultimatum… a voice without words threatening me of a last chance *(JAB!)*… I remembered Jesus was the way in from my early years so I responded fearing to be killed *(JAB!)* yet hoping for mercy. Like Job I believed God might kill me, but I have no other hope. So in fear surrendered and in fear cried out, something like 'oh Jesus come into my heart and forgive me. I need you. I don't know how or why but I know you're there. I don't know what I'm doing but I can't live without you.' I gave him all of me forever, no bargaining, no turning back, final decision. To my amazement I did not die. I didn't know what to expect next but I was just so enormously pleased to not be dead. Which is a curious thing seeing as I had been working so hard to destroy myself. I did not make sense. Not dying puzzled me but gave me a love for this God, Jesus guy. I knew this day was important and the decision was important but no clue beyond that. So on I go, the same but different. I even tell my mom on my next check in phone call. I say "mom! I'm different!" She asked "Am I gonna like it?"

We headed to the Porcupine Mountains and I got completely "don't remember anything" kind of wasted. Yet in that state I recorded in my journal "I have grown so close to God. I love him and will forever. LOVE GOD! and LOVE LIFE. Life and God are beautiful. GOD – <u>watch me always</u>!" Yup, sounds like something a person writes when they're wasted. Yet the "God guy" is my warped and maligned perception of our creator who is really "**The Pursuer**." In truth **The Pursuer** loves me beyond my capability to remotely fathom and had helped me simply because I was looking to Him. I was walking in His Grace but had no idea of it's existence. I have a long way to go before I learn of this **Pursuer** guy. We head off to Tahquamenon Falls where I have another "are you kidding me" experience. I took some mescaline before we went to the falls and decided it would be a great idea to walk from the upper falls to the lower falls. It was a four mile, treacherous, muddy, mosquito-y hike that I made more difficult because I seemed to think it was an even greater idea to walk and run next to the edge of the river instead of on the trail. I was running and talking to God and I fell in. I climbed out and continued to run sometimes in the water, sometimes on the bank, and talk to God more, oblivious to my idiocy. But like I said, He did what I asked – He kept me safe. Grace. I felt so good and noted that it must be love (Love of God). Yet danger is on the horizon and I have no idea what love really is.

Three days later in the middle of the night I read my King James Bible and Cheryl's Good News Bible and I get horrifically confused *(JAB!)*. In my infinite lack of wisdom I had chosen to read the book of Ecclesiastes and record how I am so confused on life now. I need help desperately to identify what is right and what is wrong *(JAB!)* and what is good and what is bad *(JAB!)*. I am unaware that the *"you gotta earn it"* thing *(JAB!)* is trying to throw grace out. So I go and smoke a bowl before going to sleep.

After getting back home I start going to church with my mom. She has a group of ladies there that love her and prayed for me on my trip. It's a Lutheran church close to our house. I remember my grandma went to a Lutheran church sometimes, although I had no idea what that meant. Lutheran, Baptist, Catholic… were like brands to me. What flavor you want or something. My mom's lady friends at this church had a gathering called Prayer and Praise. They would sing and pray. Seemed odd to me. My mom said that they talked about the Holy Spirit and something called tongues. My mom went to it at least once, maybe more but she was a little freaked out by it so didn't continue. Me? I had never heard of such things. I don't know if I ever went to one of those meetings but my mom bought a record album called *"The Praise Album."* I would play that over and over. It was like salve to my soul. Having been apprehended by **The Pursuer** I am in a partial state of euphoria and at the same time still quite clueless. My relationship with God is real but quite superficial due to my feelings being my compass as well as my mind and perceptions being quite negative and twisted having been tainted by *the JAB!*. But **The Pursuer** was once again setting me up to meet that Holy Spirit person thing. Sadly I missed it at that time *(JAB!)*.

In the meantime having no idea that I can control what goes on in my mind confusion goes manic in me *(JAB!)*. I discovered additional pages in the notebook I kept for my trip. They started the day after Christmas the same year **The Pursuer** apprehended me. The amount of panic and lack of identity is beyond comprehension. Who was that person? So very tormented I feel I could cry reading about her... but her, is me. Or more accurate, was me. I knew I was different then when I started this book. I knew I was messed up before. But gathering information to write my story has been quite eye opening to me as well and I am hopeful that my sharing might help someone else. Back then I remember feeling much like "the only one" in many things. The isolation was unbearable. I have come to understand that many people experience much the same things. Not necessarily identical but similar enough for overlap so we could potentially help each other. So because of that I have decided to include some of my besieged ramblings *(JAB!)*.

Bummed – thoroughly bummed.
I just don't understand
So much confusion
   What?
     God – oh God – what have you for me.
   My friends & family – nothing is the same.
Am I still me?
  Who am I?
   What am I?
    Where am I?

And...

Where am I headed

    Who is what

        What is where

            Where is who & when

You'd think I'd be on cloud 9 –

    day after Christmas

Lots of gifts

Lots of clothes after shopping this morning

Lots of people

Yet...

    I feel alone

Or if you would

Lonely

    I feel a chill

        Inside my heart

            So cold it hurts

Where...

    When...

        Why....

            Why...

                Will?

I worry – don't know why

    I'm informed I...

        Shouldn't

    There is no need

        Yet... sometimes I do.

What is going on

Where is it going

Who is it going with

Why is it going

    Will it get there

        -God Bless –

Oh the Lord is good to me

And so I thank the Lord

For giving me the things I need

I just wish I understood

-they say...

You never will

Who knows

Why do people care for other people

What reasons ly behind

The feeling

The caring

The loving

What justifies a relationship

What kind of glue

Holds it together

Crazy?

It seems so.

A yellow rose

A feeling

The meaning is imminent

Yet... Who made orange roses.

God grant me serenity

To accept the things I

Cannot change

The courage to change

Those that I can

And the wisdom to

Know the difference...

...but first I have to know

What the things are.

Maybe if I (JAB!) could get rid of all my crap

and excess Garbage

I could start over

APPREHENDED to Michael

But first I need ...a home
A.S.A.P.M.O.O.H.T.A.N.H.
(don't remember what this means)

G.S.T. (or this)

Count your blessings
 Alive fed clothed
 Warm loved God

Christmas –
 I wonder when it is – realistically

Feels so good
 To feel so here & now

HAPPY NEW YEAR – I hope
January 1st – 1979

I don't know
 My best line – I don't know
  Or even – I'm unsure

Why –
 Such "organization"
A garbage can is in better order
 I think   and I
  Contemplate and I
   Hope   and I
    Wonder and then I think again

Don't think too hard
 Your brain will explode

Words words words
 Just a bunch of letters trying to express a
  Thought or feeling

Successful?

>*I doubt it*

Well try (JAB!) try again

>*Faith as in a mustard seed*

Always present

>*No matter*

>>*How tiny*

>>>*Never forgotten*

Babble babble babble

>*I'm a brook*

Babble babble babble

>*I'm an old hag*

Babble babble babble

>*Where does it take you to...*

Oh no it hurts –

>*I forgot (help)*

My mind drifts again

>*My brain – the sail boat*

Onward

>*Upward*

>>*Outward*

>>*Inward*

>>>*Lots a words*

No sense at all

>*Or 7th sense*

>>*Nonsense*

Strange things

>*Crazy thing*

>>*All the same things*

>>*Normal things*

>>>*Who's to say   I'm not*

Work – a goal
> *Love – a feeling*
>> *What does it add up to?*
> *Add 2 + 2*
>> *I keep coming up with five*

Life goes on
> *Thank God for that*
> *I'd hate to stand still*
> *There's always God*
> *There's always hope*

(two months later)

Reading this conglomeration of thoughts
> *Is like reliving*
>> *"Go Ask Alice"*

Words   thoughts feelings

> *The blender is*
>> *On*
Someone left the top off
> *& it's making a*
>> *Terrible mess*

I (JAB!) can't seem to find the
> *Dishcloth to*
>> *Clean it up.*
> *Can't find the off switch*
>> *Or the electricity*
>>> *Has gone Haywire*
> *Where to_____*

Here?

Here?

Here?

Here?

Here?

Hear?

Schizo?

    I've been using that a lot lately.

No – not schizo –

    Just human v spirit?

        I wish the referee would stop it.

The referee must

    Get a kick out of it

        The fight goes on

Conflict_____

    Despondency_____

        Pleas_____

I call for a time out

    But I start again

        Unprepared

        Unsure

        Unconfident

        Self defeated

            Before I begin again

Keep pushin

    Keep pushin

        Keep pushin on

    Try   try   try (JAB!)

<u>*Don't*</u> *give up*

Lord I beg you

    I ask you

    I love you

        Please

Open my eyes

        Put strength in my physical being

            Stamina, will power by your will – if it be

Thank you

  Love you

    Praise you

Love the Lord thy God with all thy heart,

   all thy soul,

   all thy strength &

   all thy mind.

  The Lord is my shepherd

I must not want (JAB!)

  The Lord is my strength

   My provider

I am so glad that Jesus loves me

  Jesus loves me

   Jesus loves me

I am so glad that Jesus loves me

   Jesus love <u>even</u> me!

    What a miracle.

In the midst of all this – this vacillation, negativity, bondage, darkness, repetition of words without depth - **The Pursuer** remained faithful. He had found a way to get music back in my life even before my road trip. After much begging and explaining, my mother had agreed to buy me a guitar. She reasoned *"why bother, you'll just quit (JAB!) like you did the violin and piano."* But she was finally convinced I would make use of it, and I did. At first it became a channel to pour my negative depressing emotions *(JAB!)* through in high school. I learned sad songs and I wrote my own as well *(JAB!)*. But after **The Pursuer** apprehended me He used it as the wonderful tool He created. He used it to teach me. His patience and compassion give me pause as I write this. The songs I wrote at the beginning were so very saturated with religiousness as I tried so hard *(JAB!)* to be what I thought He wanted. My perception and knowledge of the truth were so tiny I marvel at how **The Pursuer** has done what He has in my life. Grace. My mother had a friend named Lois. Just the thought of her makes me stop to savor her positive impact on my life. I am certain this lovely lady (who is now with Jesus) has great reward for her work in my life. She changed the course of my life more than once beginning with directing me to a gathering of young people who knew Jesus. They met on Friday nights in the social hall of a Catholic church and were headed up by a guy who was a barber. How odd. I was hesitant. I mean, they met on Friday nights! Come on, that is party night! She coaxed and encouraged me to go "just once" and that I didn't ever have to go back. Choice? Hmm. Seemed harmless enough, so I went with full intention of going "just once." However I couldn't stop going. Something there kept me coming back.

3

ᘍᘏ Michael ᘍᘏ

Eventually the Friday night meeting wasn't enough for me. Even though I was still into my partying, I wanted more. I mean, my mom's church was nice and all, but I liked the music at this place better. I discovered there was a church associated with it and began to go there on Sundays. They were a nomadic kind of church – renting space and setting up each week. It was when they were meeting at S building of our local community college, that I saw him. He was there with his mom. I had known him in eighth grade. Nobody in all this church experience was anyone I had ever known before so my internal response was "someone I know!!" We had had a class assignment together. An odd thing. We had to go to the library together and read some old English romantic play for some reason I do not remember. In this play his character had a pet name for my character – cabbage. And so it was, throughout the eighth grade, whenever he would see me, he would call me cabbage and we would laugh. So apparently all of that built a familiarity in me to go up to him and reintroduce myself.

As always, **The Pursuer** was busy behind the scenes. At this point in my story I still don't recognize him as such but that doesn't stop him. He knows my condition but also that I want Him. His love is relentless and I am clueless about this thing called love. In fact, at this point in my life I had an ineffective wall around my heart built on lies *(JAB!)*. I hurt and I was angry. In that anger I declared I was "done" with men and had no intention of a romantic relationship ever. All men ever did was hurt me and leave. I concluded they were good for nothing. **The Pursuer** had other plans and proceeded to unveil them to me. I didn't see them at first, probably because I was busy drowning my angry sorrows *(JAB!)* and was not always "present" where I was at. Again, **The Pursuer** was not dissuaded. Grace.

The initial step in this plan is so subtle and completely played into my mindset at the time. By this time my previous friends didn't spend much time with me anymore so I welcomed new friends. One friend introduced me to Christian music. I had never heard of such a thing. He gave me many tapes (yes tapes – go ahead and laugh) of all different kinds of Christian music. That friend was a guy and had been nice to me and didn't require anything from me. Hmm. Another new friend at that time was a young lady who recently had received Jesus at that Friday night meeting place. She was pregnant and had health issues that prevented her from driving so I became her driver and we did many things together. At the same time my best friend from high school was getting married and I was the maid of honor. One Sunday after church in August I was headed to her house to help her with her wedding invitations and that guy I had known in eighth grade (Mike) asked me if I'd like to join him and his sister for breakfast. I had to decline his invite and I felt so bad. Why did I care so much? I was worried he thought I was lying to him and what other people thought of me was a big deal. I had that whole earning it thing going on *(JAB!)*. Anyways, I couldn't have him think I had lied so I invited him to join my new friend and I as we went to a "Revival" meeting the next day. He accepted.

And so another "are you kidding me" story begins. I pick up my friend and I pick up Mike and off we go. I started out sitting next to my friend but suddenly I was sitting next to Mike. Hmm. Following the meeting we all went to a restaurant for coffee and chatting. Afterward I take my friend home and Mike and I still have a lot to talk about so we walk around the city until four in the morning. Hmm.

Two days later we went horseback riding. We had invited others, but no one else came. Another hmm. After the church picnic four days later Mike came to my house and we had a bonfire in the back yard fire pit where I burned all my music that "wasn't Christian." More of that earn it stuff *(JAB!)*. And this Mike guy? Apparently I like him – first kiss. He had received Jesus the November before at a Clarence King rally. I could tell he was different than all the other guys I had known before. At this time he was going to church – like every day – all different churches so he could "get the Word" (huh?). The next day we went to the amusement park in Ohio that has all the roller coasters with a group of people from one of those churches. We had a great time at the park. I was both shocked and amazed by Mike reading me scripture during our wait time in the lines. He had a little Bible he carried with him. It seemed so odd but he seemed so strong. I needed strong. But wait! I had decided I was done with these people called men! Fear gripped my heart and mind *(JAB!)* and had not **The Pursuer** intervened fear would have had its way in me.

The next day I was set to go to church with my new girlfriend again. I didn't feel so good so was contemplating not going *(JAB!)*. However, **The Pursuer** intervened and at ten minutes past six in the evening I shot to my feet and out of my mouth came these words *"Just cut out your laughing and start knocking your knees. Because it's my lord in the heavens who I aim to please."* Hmm. And being suddenly fine, off to church I went. That night it finally happened. I was introduced to that Holy Spirit thing. After the service, out in the foyer they prayed for me, I fell to the ground (what the heck is that??) and after I got up they explained to me a thing called tongues. I didn't understand but I knew something was different. It was a little scary. I felt like I was making up strange noises to make them happy but perhaps they sensed my apprehension because they didn't push. Grace. They simply said to practice at home when I'm by myself. I could deal with that.

Friday arrived and Mike came to pick me up for the Friday night meeting but that fear was in the driver seat of my heart *(JAB!)*. He went to kiss me hello and I turned my head. I got in the car and proceeded to tell him the classic line we hear so much that girls say to guys "we gotta be just friends." As the words escaped my lips *(JAB!)* my heart knew those words were not true but I couldn't help myself. The fear was overwhelming *(JAB!)*. But it could not compare to the misery that followed. For the next four days I called him every day not knowing how to fix what I broke but at the same time afraid I would be able to do so. I was trapped between fears *(JAB!)*. Of course I retreated into my music. **The Pursuer** followed me there and gave me a tune without words. I never had one of those before. Hmm. On Monday Mike came over and gave me a poem he had written about me. It was a little intense about us being together.

Oddly, it went with the music **The Pursuer** had given me at precisely the same time. Hmm. (cue eerie music). Seeing it was God doing something, I wrote a comparable song in answer to it, in addition to one called "Make Me Understand" which was me talking to God.

The next day was Tuesday and I called Mike again, like I had the previous three days. So we talked for an hour and then he suddenly said bye and hung up. AHH!! God help me!! I tried to fix it!! On Tuesday evenings Mike went to a gathering called The Breadline. I knew I had to go. What was I going to do? So I threw myself on God crying out for help - I had done *(JAB!)* all I knew to do and came up empty. Although I had no idea what "having faith" was I had every expectation that God would take care of it. I mean, "He started it" I felt. It only made sense. I was not aware that it is written in the Bible that He would do just that. In fact, it can be found in more than one place. Come around six o'clock I started pacing around the house and my mom was asking me why. I just expected to go even though I didn't know how. I knew that Mike left around six thirty and as that time passed I still paced. Sometime after six thirty and before seven the phone rang and it was Mike asking me if I wanted to go to The Breadline. I said yes of course and he came and picked me up. During that evening everyone there was instructed to get in a circle, join hands and that is when **The Pursuer** fixed what I broke and had no power to repair. That is actually the core of what is known as the gospel – **The Pursuer** fixed what was broken (our relationship with him) which we had no power to repair (His blood for ours). He joined us back together with "the Word." Reconciled by Jesus. Likewise here, as the pastor read from the book of *Ephesians* chapter four, **The Pursuer** graciously engraved it on my soul. The pastor read the King James Version and certain words rang out "walk worthy of the vocation where with you are called" and "forbearing one another in love." **The Pursuer** translated to my soul what he desired for me and reassured me that it would be good. I needed to take what I was so afraid of and trust Him with it, take up this relationship as a career, a calling and put up with some stuff I didn't like because there will always be something I won't like. Somehow I knew that if I did, everything would be ok. Of course, no details, no promises given. Just something inside me knew. So I made the decision to trust. Grace.

Mike's family had been involved with a more hands on kind of group through their church and went to a special summer camp. This particular year Mike was going for the entire time while his mom and sister were to join him later. After that night at The Breadline **The Pursuer** (who I often referred to as "Lord," meaning boss) was involved in my music and strengthening me in my obedience to this relationship. I knew I was going to miss Mike while he was gone. But it wouldn't be for too long as I had been invited to accompany his mom and sister at the latter part of camp. Before Mike left for the camp I gave him a card to open later in which I confessed that I loved him because the Lord told me. Real romantic eh? Hey, I had no idea how to run my life and had always given someone or something outside of myself the power. Internal freedom was not something I had any idea of. **The Pursuer** used my broken parts to help me. Two days after he left for camp I wrote a song in response to what I "knew" inside. Somehow I "knew" God wanted us "together" and in writing that song Mike became forever Michael in my heart. Early into the next day at exactly 1:01am – 1:03am **The Pursuer** did something I had never encountered before. **The Pursuer** wrote lyrics to a song and I was the awestruck one holding the pen. He then continued to complete the music by 1:22

am and proceeded to inform me that I am to sing this to Michael…
along with that other song I wrote. *Seriously?? (JAB!) No! I'm not
doing that!! Are you crazy?.... blah blah blah…..* until I finally
submitted. I agreed to do it even though it terrified me. Somehow I
trusted this "Lord."

Be My Rainbow

© Danielle Bernock 1979

Let the Son Shine
He gave me you
Covenants He does make
Be my rainbow

During the storm
The Lord doth come
He calms it down
And makes us one
Be my rainbow

The Lord made a promise
To all the earth
No longer to wash us away
We trust in that
And in each other
Be the covenant God gave me
Be the covenant God gave us
Please be my rainbow

Let the Son shine
He gave me you
Be my rainbow

Could **you** do this thing I was being asked to do? I didn't know how I was going to do it but made a decision to do that trust thing believing somehow someway God would help me. Grace. Here I was again with that "you started it" thing. It felt like an assignment I had to complete but apparently I had some of that faith stuff I knew nothing about because I fully expected God to make this impossible thing possible. Grace. Again, no details given, no promises known. Two days later I completed my assignment and **The Pursuer** completed his twenty seven day plan. It was all so messy and neat at the same time. I sang the songs, Michael proposed and we were "engaged" – just like that. And then, we sat on the blanket on the ground bewildered with what had just happened and what we were doing and these new words – ahhh!! "engaged" "fiancé" "bride" "groom".... we had no ring... what are we going to tell people??... Stunned, we decided to keep it a secret, at least for now. However, **The Pursuer** apparently had no intention of keeping it secret. As we walked to the mess hall the next meal Michael's mother starts crying and saying stuff like "I'm losing my baby." Michael and I look at each other stunned and whisper the accusation that the other had told. Neither of us had and so we kept right on holding our secret in. We were unprepared to address this. After camp when Michael dropped me off at home my mother asked me "so when are you announcing your engagement?" AHHHHHH!!!! I asked her "who told you?" She said "the Lord did." That was amazing, comforting and disturbing all in one. Apparently **The Pursuer** wanted us to be certain so He added even another. When we went to The Breadline the next time we simply asked the pastor if he would pray with us and he responded with "you guys are getting married." Of course we asked how he knew and he had the same answer my mom had given me. We no longer had any doubts of the decision so we presented ourselves to Michael's parents to make our announcement. Their response was justified and amusing. We told them we were getting married because "the Lord" was telling us to and they asked us "do you love each other?" We paused, looked at each other and said in unison "I guess so." Not your usual ride off into the sunset love story but it was just the beginning of **The Pursuer's** work. He had so much more planned than we could have dreamed. We began our relationship quite supernaturally, awkwardly following the instructions that seemed so foreign to us. But as we continued, we fell quite in love with one another.

4

❧ Only the Beginning ❧

As I write this it has now been thirty three years and Michael and I are quite "joined at the hip" as the saying goes. We love each other more now than at the beginning. We love each other differently also because we "know" each other more, as in we have "learned" one another. And we have both grown. The road I have traveled has been both wonderful and messy. **The Pursuer** provided all the wonderful and I provided all the messy. His grace had no fear of our mess. What I thought about him, how I "saw" him didn't change who He was. It only stifled my ability to receive all His wonderfulness. He, **The Pursuer**, IS LOVE. So even though my limitations stifled me, He always would find a way. He loves us so much.

I have learned that I am a visual person. I learn best by seeing instead of simply hearing. And when they are combined it becomes a demonstration. The lies that tormented my inner life were laid using sight and sound, situations or experiences. The lies were demonstrated *(JAB!)*. And to accentuate that, they were demonstrated during my childhood, my formative years *(JAB!) (JAB!)*. So why is this important? Because the man **The Pursuer** gave me to marry was a visual of God's unconditional and never abandoning love for me. He was a demonstration of the opposite of an inner wounding that I was unaware of at that time. Just like it said in the song **The Pursuer** wrote about the rainbow being the visual of the promise, my husband was my visual. **The Pursuer** was using his strongest, unfailing weapon – unconditional LOVE. And he was doing it with skin on.

Back during the "pairing" of Michael and I, my love for God was very real while at the same time my view of what he was like was very religious, very harsh and very much rooted in behavioral requirements. His gracious mercy experientially "pursued" me all the way to California and back until He apprehended me. I didn't understand the unconditional love that moved him to do that. I had never seen it before. Never heard of it before. They certainly didn't teach me that at that church when I was a kid *(JAB!)*. There was always something I had to do, some condition, some qualifying behavior or response *(JAB!)*. Growing up, love had always been conditional *(JAB!)*. I knew duty, responsibility, obligation, earning, manipulation, intimidation aka fear. This love thing was foreign to my understanding but I wanted more of it. Erroneously believing *(JAB!)* it had to cost me something I vacillated between love and fear constantly. I read about how a God guy aka Jesus who loved me but then I read about a "slothful servant" who gets thrown into outer darkness. OMG! That was absolutely terrifying to me *(JAB!)*. I didn't know what outer darkness was but I was pretty sure it wasn't anything I wanted any part of. That fear drove me to do so many things *(JAB!)*. It also tainted my understanding of **The Pursuer's** plan in our pairing *(JAB!)*. I initially believed the lie *(JAB!)* that because God went to such extremes to put us together surely there was some grand reason why. Something was required of us *(JAB!)*. Some ginormous task we must complete, position we must attain, ministry we must start... to pay him back or earn what He had given *(JAB!)*. It was almost like I was given something on credit and had to spend my life to pay it back. More of that *"earn it"* stuff. It took me many years to understand and freely accept that He paired us simply because He loved us and **The Pursuer** was patient with my process. Although because of my incorrect view, *the JAB!* had access to both my mind and my circumstances to mess things up. However because **The Pursuer** IS who He is - LOVE, He never left me or failed to help me, even though my expectations were skewed by that unworthy I didn't deserve it thing *(JAB!)*. Still He did what He does, He pursued me - anyways. Grace.

I didn't know anything about what is referred to as "walking by faith" or even heard of it, even though that was what we had done. I was thankful and I wanted to make this God happy who had done so much for me. And I also wanted to stay out of that outer darkness. I had bought the lies *the JAB!* had sold me and very little of what I believed about **The Pursuer** hadn't been tainted by them. So if I believed God wanted me to do something, you could be pretty certain that I would do it. It's not that I didn't love this God who saved me, it was more like I had no accurate knowledge of His grace and no clue what love really was. It is amazing how **The Pursuer** accepted my teeny tiny bit of faith and did such amazing things. Things like this man He gave me who loved me in a way I never knew before. I told this guy all the gory details of my past that I could remember just to try to make him go away before I got attached to him. Yet, he stayed. So regarding love? First I was happy to not be dead which is what I believed I deserved. And now I was given this man that actually **chose** to love me, the good, the bad and the ugly – forever, which I knew I did not deserve. Those things were huge to me and created a response of devotion to the one who provided them, the God who saved me, but I was very unstable due to the immense amount of fear that was a part of who I was. I did not, but **The Pursuer** knew why, and He poured out more grace.

Weddings nowadays are such a huge thing. So much invested in a single day. Sometimes becoming the entire focus eclipsing the relationship itself. We didn't have that problem. Many others, but not that one. We addressed the issue of "forever" or "as long as you both shall live" many weeks before the ceremony privately vowing to each other. It made the wedding a mere formality to us in many ways. We were in a hurry to leave our yucky past behind and naively get to the happily ever after part. We had a small wedding and simple reception. I purchased a regular dress for twenty dollars and wore ballet slippers. We had little money. I had even less self value. The thought of purchasing an official wedding dress to be worn one time was outside the scope of my mind *(JAB!)*.

My husband and I had discussed it before we were married and we agreed we were not going to have children for numerous reasons. One reason being we had both been told we probably couldn't have children *(JAB!)*. So why get your hopes up anyways. And then there was the fear of having deformed children due to all the drugs in our past *(JAB!)*. And also there was the fear of the ability to raise children properly and not screw them up *(JAB!)*. So we in no way trusted ourselves. Then stir in some end time theology and all the fear *(JAB!)* that went with it which was very popular at that time. If that were not enough I had read something in the Bible that only intensified all that fear. In my numerous times of reading the Bible only to avoid sinning (as I explained earlier) I had read many scriptures that started with *"woe unto..."* that I applied to myself *(JAB!)*. But this particular one instilled the fear of being pregnant, giving birth and nursing all placed inside that popular end time stuff going around *(JAB!)*. Talk about fear *(JAB!)* of being a mother. However **The Pursuer** IS LOVE and has NO fear in Him. He had plans to prosper me, not harm me, to help me, not hurt me. It didn't matter to Him that we considered ourselves completely undeserving and unqualified or that I was afraid. He simply dismissed that other scripture and directed my attention to Psalm 113 where it said *"He raises up the poor out of the dust, and lifts the needy out of the dunghill; That he may set him with princes, even with the princes of his people. He makes the barren woman to keep house, and to be a joyful mother of children. Praise ye the LORD"* I didn't understand the whole thing – especially the princes part. I couldn't even see myself in a regular wedding dress – what's this princes stuff? But I understood the barren woman thing and I liked the joyful part. It sounded good and I knew it was from the God who saved me so I received it. He told me of two amazing children with accompanying names He planned and set aside just for us. A boy and a girl. Seriously?? Yes. He began revealing this to me on our honeymoon. It was just as supernatural as our pairing. So much so that I considered perhaps they were our grandiose thing we were to do to justify being paired together. That was the answer! We were going to be these amazing parents, not making any of the mistakes our parents made, raising them... blah blah blah. Yeah right, just like I was going to be that research biologist. But **The Pursuer** in His amazingness could use anything we gave him to work good in our lives, even our naivety and foolishness. So, accepting His blessing yet being clueless of what we were getting ourselves into we sat down and prayed to receive these two children and were given their names, Nathan and Naomi. Not long after that I discovered I was pregnant. It was so surreal.

Surreal turned to reality when pregnancy and I were not friends. The only thing I enjoyed about pregnancy was feeling the wonder of my child moving within me, their amazing life. That part I loved deeply. I loved them deeply. But between the fear that drove me and the hormones that raged I was a complete emotional basket case. Many times I said my husband deserved a medal for simply staying with me. There he was, being that demonstration. I would have left me if I could have found a way. I even tried one time, walking seven miles from my house to my mother in laws house. But where ever I go, there I am. I knew beyond a shadow of a doubt that this child that I adored was a gift from God yet because of my fear *(JAB!)* and lack of knowing the God who saved me as **The Pursuer** *(JAB!)* my mind drew horrid pictures of evil possibilities *(JAB!)*. Still **The Pursuer** provided for us and protected both me and my precious baby even when *the JAB!* tried to steal both our lives the week before delivery.

When we were first married we lived in a lovely yet small upper flat with an amazing landlady, Mrs. Brady, who gave me great advice and made me lemon poppy seed bread. I loved going downstairs to chat with her. She advised me to get up with my husband every day and always wave goodbye to him as he goes to work. I am thankful I listened to her. This habit has been a good thing. She is such a sweet memory to me similar to my grandmother.

When we needed a larger place because of the baby **The Pursuer** set us up with a lovely little house we rented. It was perfect. Well as perfect as it could be for me the basket case. And then *the JAB!* did a direct onslaught hidden quite cunningly inside human wisdom and logic. I was seven months pregnant and my husband was offered a promotion. I know, that sounds wonderful, especially because we were struggling financially. Problem was it was in another state. Second problem is that they wanted an answer the same day *(JAB!)*. The answer should have been no, but on the advice from the authority figures in our lives who all said it was an "opportunity of a lifetime," to our harm we said yes.

So we celebrated Thanksgiving in October, canceled the baby shower, packed up our perfect little house in a moving truck towing our little white car we called the bug and headed to Minneapolis. It was supposed to be an adventure and joy. It did not play out that way. It proved to be a mistake of colossal proportions *(JAB!)*. I, the pregnant emotional basket case, was cooped up in a hotel room for two weeks without a car eating the free donuts for breakfast, fast food for lunch and going out to a local eatery for onion rings with mustard at one in the morning or later just to see my husband who was working eighteen hour or so days. I had horrendous heartburn stopped only by milkshakes. Not the diet any OBGYN with a brain would suggest. We were allotted one day to go out and find a place to live *(JAB!)*. We were not successful. I wrote horrifically sad songs and wallowed in self-pity *(JAB!)* having absolutely no clue it was self-pity *(JAB!)*. All I felt was thrashing, writhing, tormenting pain and had no idea a solution existed let alone how to implement it. Looking back I see such a pathetic sort of person so bound by lies she sat imprisoned in an open cage. I shake my head in amazement that **The Pursuer** didn't give up on me and cast me out – but He is what He is in spite of what we think or believe – He IS LOVE, He is **The Pursuer.** His love is unfailing, His grace abounding.

After two weeks we discussed our situation and came to see that this had indeed been the wrong decision *(JAB!)*. Yet, here we are. What are we going to do? Discussing the terrible options available we made the hard decision to return back home. This cost my husband his job *(JAB!)* and his reputation *(JAB!)*. The house we had previously been renting had not been rented to someone else yet so we were permitted to return to that same house. Grace. I don't remember how we paid for the trip back home. Grace. We returned with no job and no insurance for the baby. Embarrassed, humiliated, confused are only some of the words that describe how we felt. When was that happily ever after going to start? I mean, all this supernatural leading and we are here? But due to ignorance *(JAB!)* it gets worse.

Due to our erratic circumstances I didn't have an OBGYN and ended up going through the clinic at the hospital because they would "work with us" on the financial end. My due date was not known due to my erratic cycle. I was sent downtown to the health department and sent for an amniocentesis which was terrifying and unsuccessful. I got due dates from Thanksgiving to February. To top it off, at my weekly doctor visit they hospitalized me for something called pre-eclampsia *(JAB!)* but was released after a couple days when the blood pressure went down. I really had no clue what that was or how serious it could have been. With what I know now it is very evident **The Pursuer** intervened and saved my precious baby and me. Now I know how deadly it can be. Then on Christmas Eve morning I saw the doctor I "usually" saw at the clinic. He stated that I'd go until at least the New Year and then he went on vacation. However, later that day my water started to leak. The hospital said to come right in. We choose to celebrate Christmas with our families first. Apparently the people working there on Christmas were very unhappy to be there. Between their attitudes and my ignorance *(JAB!)* it was a most unpleasant experience. Some doctor I never knew delivered my precious daughter. Unfortunately I was not very present in the moment having been given drugs to make me unconscious during labor and then a saddle block for delivery. I adored this precious little soul, but I didn't know anything about being a mom. Why did **The Pursuer** trust me with this precious beautiful life? Because He loves – it's what He does – it's what He is. I had no accurate perception of this at the time. It didn't dissuade Him. He planned to teach me. Grace teaches.

After this we continued to have financial difficulties and ended up on unemployment and government assistance *(JAB!)*. I never had that baby shower so we had very little and everything we had was second hand. My mom had saved some things that she gave to us. So we had a bassinet, a crib and a play pen (yes play pen – the wooden slat kind). And then **The Pursuer** steps in again with an abundance beyond my fathoming. A lady from where we were going to church approached me stating she had lots of stuff left from her daughter if I wanted it. OMG! What a plethora of provision!! I believe it was eleven or twelve garbage bags full of everything I needed and more. In addition to clothing she gave me a swing, bouncy seat etc. It was amazing. I had no money to purchase anything and in these bags of clothing were things I wouldn't have dreamed to have for my baby girl. I could change her clothes just for fun! Remember I couldn't bring myself to buy a wedding gown for myself. Yet here for my daughter this abundance is wonderful and welcomed. **The Pursuer** is demonstrating His daddy heart and I am beyond thankful yet that positive daddy thing, toward me, escaped me at the time. I could easily see it toward my baby girl. I saw how her daddy loved her. But I excluded myself *(JAB!)*. I apparently had daddy issues *(JAB!)* and was not ready to face them yet.

I knew that we were told two children but that pregnancy and delivery was no fun at all. Plus I got it wrong in that I thought I was going to have a boy. *Isn't that what the God who saved me said? (JAB!) How do I know He even talked to me? (JAB!) How can I trust to go through that again? (JAB!) Did I make it all up? (JAB!)* But **The Pursuer** intervened again. The love that wooed was irresistible even though I didn't understand it at all. I still remember the moment I surrendered. Twenty two months after my daughter was born I gave birth to my precious son just like **The Pursuer** said. Although pregnancy and I were never friends, I fully enjoyed the wonder of his precious life inside of me moving and kicking. I loved him so intensely. It was a wonder filled thing, like that song when I was a kid *(when I in awesome wonder, consider...)*. We also did have more stable circumstances for this pregnancy so I had my own OBGYN who was so gentle and kind. I had learned from my previous experience and armed myself with information. Back when my daughter was born, it was the time when "going natural" to give birth was the popular thing. Of course because I wanted to "belong" that is what I attempted to do and miserably failed *(JAB!)*. This time I learned about things called epidurals and was able to be present in the moment and watch this amazing moment, my precious son be born. It was so amazing that afterward I remember saying "that was fun, I could do that again." Such joy! Just like that scripture *"joyful mother of children."* Now I had both of the promised children **The Pursuer** had designed for me. Both of them came healthy and whole. Both of them carried middle names that cried out for the grace I knew I needed. Such immense gratitude and joy, yet that pervasive fear sat in the back of my mind like a monster that would rage when poked *(JAB!)*. I cherished and adored my children and I never wanted my children to ever doubt they were wanted and loved like the thoughts had plagued me. More than anything else I wanted to be a good mom. Surely the God who saved me would help me.

Not too long after our son was born our landlords told us their daughter needed the house so we would have to move by the end of June *(JAB!)*. Where were we going to go? We were barely getting along. We used some of our food stamps to buy pop just so we could get the deposit back to buy toilet paper. We had no money for moving. At least we had been given a few months heads up. We were thankful for that. In the meantime close friends of ours discovered some townhouses that were co-ops. We looked into them and got ourselves on the waiting list even though the wait was six months to a year and we would need a chunk of money. We didn't have the money and the time frame was very iffy. Of course we prayed and then hoped. What else could we do? Again – enter **The Pursuer.** A couple from the church we were a part of had bought a new house and were moving. But there was a space in their timeline where the house they had sold would be vacant. They offered us to live there for that time. How awesome is that?! Somehow **The Pursuer** caused us to not be bothered by the location of this house or the reason they moved. This house was in a declining area of Detroit and they moved due to crime in the neighborhood. We simply prayed and expected to be safe and we were. Grace. There's that walking by faith thing again that I didn't understand but it somehow would kick in here and there. The day after we moved out, the house across the street was broken into. We were well aware that the God who saved us had protected us there. And not only that but we moved from there right into those townhouses in just five months! Grace. But not before *the JAB!* struck again.

My husband had been in school and doing roofing jobs with a friend all summer when a new opportunity came along. They both got hired into a real company to do the same work for more money! Praise God! We were both so very excited as we saw a light at the end of the tunnel of poverty. Then it happened. I get a phone call from Detroit Receiving Hospital asking me if I am Mrs. Bernock *(JAB!).* Talk about fear. The lady informed me that my husband had been brought there by ambulance. He had fallen two stories, injured his back and had a compound fracture in his leg in three places, needed surgery and was lucky he was not dead *(JAB!).* Wow! This was their first job! Apparently the ladder holding the scaffold broke and they both fell. Statistics said one of them should have died. But **The Pursuer** intervened and altered those statistics. They both were alive. Injured severely but alive. We liked alive.

I was very thankful to say the least. But **The Pursuer** looking for every opportunity to reveal His love was not finished. He took this awful *(JAB!)* and turned it into a positive. I have since seen Him do this over and over again which is very much in agreement with who He is – **The Pursuer.** However, some people say He causes the bad so He can do these good things. And even though that makes no sense and no normal human would do that, somehow *the JAB!* is convincing in his selling of this lie. I know, there were times when I bought it. How awful to have your character constantly vilified. But He knew I still knew Him as the God who saved me and not **The Pursuer** and His love was not altered by my ignorance. Grace. So instead of this situation destroying us in all the ways *the JAB!* had planned, it did quite the opposite. Having been hired by a real company, there was insurance and workman's comp. This took care of the medical bills and provided us with more income than we had ever had before that. Our friends and family blessed us in many ways. They babysat so I could be at the hospital. When Michael came home he had a cast from toe to upper thigh and we were given a chair that was like a chaise lounge for him. One friend took me grocery shopping. Another friend brought us his video game system to use to curb boredom. Both of our birthdays are in August and my husband's fall occurred the day before my birthday so our family threw us a surprise birthday party with all our friends after he came home from the hospital. Not long after this the time came that we got the phone call from the townhouse complex that a unit was available. The timeframe worked out perfect but we didn't have the deposit required. **The Pursuer** provided again. A loan was given and later even forgiven and we moved in with much help from family and friends.

I see **The Pursuer** there so clearly now. I did not back then. He was the God who saved me and that was awesome. But that conditional, or obligation thing *(JAB!)* sat back there with the fear monster *(JAB!)*. They *(JAB!)* even tried to get us to do another one of those ginormous mistakes again like Minneapolis. Even shrouded it in "serving God" and we almost took the bait. We applied to a ministry in another state and got accepted. Yet something inside us was just not comfortable with following through so we canceled. *The JAB!* was foiled. I learn later this is something called "inward witness." Good thing we didn't need to know these religious terms to walk in them. Yay! We are actually learning something and my first glimpse of **The Pursuer** is on the horizon.

After moving we visited with our old neighbor Dee a few times. Dee loved us and our kids and we loved her back. On one of our visits she told us about a relative of hers, a little boy that needed serious prayer to stay alive. His name was Brian Miller. He was only two, had a heart defect and was going to have surgery to install a device that had not been done before on anyone so young.

This story touched my heart deeply and **The Pursuer** capitalized upon it to begin to open my eyes. This little boy was on my mind and heart and in my prayers in an intense way unlike any before. I prayed for this little boy and he lived. This impacted me very deeply. God heard me! The God who saved me heard ME! It was as if **The Pursuer** was undoing the lie that gained access when I had prayed for my grandmother and she died. I wrote a song for Brian filled with expectation of Love from God. This experience left a mark somewhere new in me that this love I wrote about for Brian might actually be for me also. But how is that so? I'm "saved," of course God loves me. This was different. I did not fully understand it, yet it left a mark forever. A good mark. A love mark. A light that revealed the love of **The Pursuer.** It was another step in the process of the undoing of that bull's-eye I was unaware had occurred.

A few months later I started to write in an attempt to communicate better with the God who saved me. I didn't know how to talk to him, which is interesting because back when He first apprehended me I didn't seem to have this problem. What happened between then and here? I would ask him WHY was I so fearful. I wrote about verses in the Bible taking me in circles, accusing thoughts, fear of *"falling into outer darkness,"* relating to and quoting an old song I wrote in junior high called *"Confusion" (JAB!)* Something is going on and I am clueless to what IT is. Meanwhile my faithful husband has been completing his schooling. And right here, in the midst of my darkness **The Pursuer** graciously provides again. Michael graduated from college with two associates degrees successfully changing his vocation from what took us to Minneapolis and what almost took his life in that accident. This blessing from **The Pursuer** begins taking our lives in a new direction. Another new direction is that my mother and I begin tearing down walls and building a friendship that grows beyond our dreams.

5

The Pit, The Hole, The Process
ℰↄন

So much positive change. So much blessing. So much love in our home. I am so thankful. I love going to that place called church. I love my family. I know they love me and I belong there! They are my happy place. One would think I now see that the God who saved me was **The Pursuer** who passionately loves me and that he is so gracious and faithful. But *the JAB!* had successfully built a fortress of darkness with lies and fear in my mind. They hide in the back of my mind when the light of truth is shining and come out to argue in private using the pain that planted them. My mind is horribly negative. I have no grasp on what is going on inside my head or that I have the power to control it. The grace that pursued me out to California and back, as well as the supernatural pairing is perverted by *the JAB!* demanding proper behavior as if I needed pay God back. As if that were even possible. Ridiculous. The grace **The Pursuer** has for us, the crown of His creation, is unmerited which means we cannot earn it. It is not possible. Yet *the JAB!* gives voice to "the law" wherever possible setting impossible requirements, obligations, duties. Hearing I had to "work out my own salvation" and *"take up my cross"* meant that God did his part with his grace by apprehending me and it was now my responsibility to prove to God I was worth His effort *(JAB!)*. I try and succeed some and fail more. I call myself wretched. I see my sin constantly. I focus on the negative in me and my mistakes because I believe I am expected to fix it.

I write to God in my journal: *"My mind is a battle ground of voices shouting what to do (JAB!). I feel like it's out of some horror flick. I don't know how to make it stop. I've begged you to – but – nothing. Why do you let me be tortured so? So many questions. I'm afraid of my questions. I'm afraid of the answers. I feel like a dirty old abandoned animal cowering in some alley, afraid of its shadow. I want desperately for someone to find me, yet rebuke is my portion (JAB!). Do I have to rescue myself? I don't know if that is even possible. I feel so bad for my family. Especially Michael. There is no way they can know what is going on inside. They just see pain. They don't understand. They, like me, just want it to go away. I don't want to get on the roller coaster in my head so I remain numb. Scripture after scripture. I thought the Word was to give life…make the lies go away. I'm afraid of myself…I don't want to talk. I only trust you. Not even my own voice. My tongue would betray me. I just want to sit and wait for you or die…If I could die from sorrow. With what I can, I love you. With all I have, I cling to you. Master – tell me what to do."*

That is some serious depression and self-condemnation. Although I hear the message of the love of God it always seems to have some "but" attached to it when it comes to me. I can see he loves others. Especially my children. I never had a doubt how precious to him they are and tell them constantly. I even made up a little good morning song for them that declared how much I love them and how Jesus loved them even more than I loved them. For them to know they are loved was paramount to me. But somehow I exclude myself with the only hope offered being rooted in something I must do. And I work harder and do a lot of good yet fear that it is not enough *(JAB!)*. So much confusion followed by condemnation because I'm not supposed to be confused but then I condemn myself for that. I keep trying to be what I think I'm supposed to be but then I'm not sure what I'm supposed to be anyways. This leads me to being afraid that God will give up on me which leads me to only try harder. Until **The Pursuer** rescued me.

A Man Fell in A Pit Story

A man fell into a pit and couldn't get himself out.
A subjective person came along and said, "I feel for you down there."
An objective person came along and said, "Well, it's logical that someone would fall down there."
Confucius said, "If you would have listened to me you wouldn't be in that pit."
Buddha said, "Your pit is only a state of mind."
A Christian scientist came along and said, "You only THINK that you're in that pit."
A Pharisee said, "Only bad people fall into pits."
A mathematician calculated how he fell into the pit.
A professor gave him a lecture on the elementary principles of the pit.

A scientist calculated the pressure necessary, pounds and square
inches, to get him out of the pit.
An evolutionist said, "You will die in the pit so you can't
produce any more pit-falling offspring."
A news reporter wanted an exclusive story on his pit.
A fundamentalist said, "You deserve your pit."
A Calvinist said, "If you had been saved, you would have never
fallen into that pit."
A Wesleyan said, "You were saved and still fell into that pit."
A charismatic said, "Just confess that you are not in that pit."
A realist said, "Now THAT'S A PIT."
A geologist told him to appreciate the rock strata in the pit.
An IRS man asked if he was paying taxes on his pit.
The county inspector asked if he had a permit to dig the pit.
An evasive person came along and avoided the subject
altogether.
A self-pitying person said, "You haven't seen MY pit."
An optimist said, "Things could be worse."
A pessimist said, "Things will get worse."

Jesus seeing the man reached down and took him by the
hand and lifted him out of the pit.

-author unknown

In this pit I start to develop physical symptoms. Oh no!
It's deja vu all over again. In high school my mom took me to the
Emergency Room numerous times for severe intestinal pain. They
always sent me home without any help and discounting the
reality of my pain. She also took me over to Canada to some
special kind of Chiropractor for the same issues and got some

measure of comfort yet no cure. Doctors never came up with a diagnosis, they said I was making it up, "it was all in my head" *(JAB!)*. They were both right and wrong. All those lies, fears and losses were never addressed and so they manifested themselves physically. It is something called somatization. It is the conversion of mental experiences or emotions into bodily symptoms.

This time was similar yet different. I had completely different symptoms. I had the sensation that my "brain was melting." My belly would spontaneously blow up like a balloon, turn rock hard and hurt like it was going to burst. People would ask me if I was pregnant when that happened. I would need to change clothes when it occurred so I brought an alternate set everywhere I went to change into. The "brain melting" sensation affected my already messed up thinking. I explored possible food allergies and got numerous tests that showed nothing. No doctor identified the cause for approximately three years. During those years I got the same accusations and demoralizing responses I got as a teenager that fed my feelings of worthlessness *(JAB!)*. But this time I also had a religious spin going also. In my journal I wrote: *"I am sore afflicted. My body pains. Pain within, pain without. Be my comfort. This inside pain in my guts – will it ever leave me? This pain in my heart, grief, it eats me up. Have I sinned oh God. Show me if I be guilty, that confess I might be healed. Thy will. Thy will. Not my will...."* And then I ask God to help me not blaspheme if this is the state I must live in – thinking this vile thing might be his will *(JAB!!!!!)*.

One day while driving my kids to school I got ever so gently rear ended at a red light. It was so slight I didn't even get out of the car to address it. I figured no harm no foul. Until I got home and suddenly my neck went into a rage of pain. I went to the nearest chiropractor and it was confirmed whiplash. This chiropractor was great. He not only took care of me for the whiplash but did what the other doctors could not do. After a few visits and discussions he identified my problem. He gave me a book called *"Missing Diagnosis."* It was all about me! I finally felt validated. I wasn't making it up – it was real. It was about a physical condition called Candidiasis that many doctors were still unwilling to validate. I then read the book *"The Yeast Connection: A Medical Breakthrough."* This led me to a doctor who gave me a prescription for Nystatin and I found relief. That was until **The Pursuer** was able to show me a more excellent way – complete healing.

After the diagnosis I started counseling to address my past that was "leaking" into my present. It helped some. That is where I learned that fancy word for how I processed emotions in high school. The counselor had me keep a journal – in it I say hysteria is hiding, I express anguish, intense pain, despair, fear, shame. This counselor instructs me to write down what I want from God and how I want him to treat this afflicted, hurt, rejected, abandoned part of me. Then he tells me the story of the shepherd with the hundred sheep – ninety nine safe and one lost – can I feel special? My answer was no with tears. I thought that only applied evangelistically.

I ask *"Is there hope of being precious in His sight?"* I hate myself. I state I don't know what God means when he says he loves me. I want God to make me believe love. I want God to change my perception of him to truth. I express I want to believe God but don't. His promises are like mirages in the desert – the counselor points it out as sin *(JAB!)*. I feel trapped and say *"I cannot win"* but the counselor labels it as quitting *(JAB!)*. My soul is in a "frenzy." I say *"I am nothing. I can have nothing. I can give nothing. In the judgment I expect nothing. There is no purpose for pain or life. God makes my life hard but I thought he came to set me free."* The counselor, missing the core problem, tells me to read the Bible and take God at his word. Ok sure. More stuff to do *(JAB!)* and off I go trying more.

I wanted to be well. I wanted to be happy. But then I ran into trouble with that because "wanting" things had been tied to sin and selfishness *(JAB!)*. Both of which were bad. Hence all the "if it be your will" praying. But I knew that God did heal. I just didn't know if I could qualify. In the Bible I found something I could do. It says that if there is any sick to call the elders of the church, have them pray and anoint with oil. So that is what we did. Sadly I left unaffected perceiving they had no more faith than I did. I really wanted to believe. There is that "want" thing again *(JAB!)*, like a speed bump in the road. Yet, **The Pursuer** has the answer in motion in spite of my lack of understanding and inability to believe this stuff could actually be for me – because he loves me. Even there in the pit. He reaches in and pulls me out.

We were at a team meeting for a new company we became involved with at someone's house. We were new to the organization. At this meeting a gentleman I didn't know approached me and said he felt God wanted him to give me this particular book called *"New Thresholds of Faith."* I devoured and studied this book learning that I could indeed be healed and how. The book changed my life. This organization changed my life. New ways of thinking were being formed. I learned something about attitude that I had not ever been able to grasp before. I learned I have power. I, me, yes me, I can control this thing called attitude. Not an instant thing I master but a new process begins. Someone else in the organization brings a book into my life called *"What To Say When You Talk To Yourself."* This book brought such a dramatic change. Speaking to yourself on purpose seemed silly. Especially one example they gave to say cracked us up. We still joke about that line. I made myself a "self-talk" tape (yes tape, go ahead and laugh) that I played for a season. It felt weird but it did help. So much change going on in our lives, including a change in where we went to church. I got my hands on yet another book that brought light and power into my life called *"The Authority of the Believer."* One Sunday the pastor at this new place spoke about being healed and was asking people to come up to the front for prayer. I had been studying that book on faith and really looking at how to have what it said. So when the pastor was doing this, in my heart I looked to the Lord and asked him if it was time. It was like I was talking to **The Pursuer** again but didn't know it. His grace is so elegant. I didn't get any kind of verbal answer but it just "seemed" like it was time. So I went up there, paying attention more to the Lord than the pastor that prayed for me and then I went back to my seat. No fanfare, no goose bumps. Inside I just felt like "ok, what's next." When we got home it was time for me to take my medicine. I took it out of the cupboard and hesitated remembering my question to the Lord. So again I looked to the Lord and asked if I should take it or not. Again, no verbal stuff just that "thing" inside to trust. I was a little scared but the desire to trust was stronger so I went with that. I never took it again. I was completely healed. According to the books that helped me identify the problem, it was a chronic problem with no cure. I guess **The Pursuer** didn't read those books. In fact he went beyond healing. He desires wholeness so he proceeded to teach me what the pit was. He illustrated it as a different kind of somatization. Jesus had warned his disciples to beware of the leaven of the Pharisees. My misdirected effort focused on behavior turned me into a law minded Pharisee when I was seeking to be a dedicated servant. I was horrified. **The Pursuer** was not. The only condemnation I experienced was self-inflicted. **The**

Pursuer was full of compassion and simply continued his process of changing how I see him, as well as changing how I see myself.

"There's a Hole in my Sidewalk" by Portia Nelson illustrates the process beautifully. This QR code will take you to her poem.

6

❧❧Ch-Ch-Ch-Ch-Changes↩↩

Ch-Ch-Ch-Ch-Changes! Big time changes. Among the many, the largest by far is the legal changing of my name. It is so ginormous that I am shocked to be unable to find any record of me charting it along the way. Perhaps I do have some notes and simply put them in a "nice safe place where I won't lose them." Ever done that? Maybe I'll find them after I complete this book and wish I would have included some details. Too bad. I have realized that what is in this book will be incomplete and my views subject to change because I am growing and growing things change. Who I am today as I write this is a very different person than who I was at this point in my story. There are things I believed and were convinced were true I disagree with now. So note to you my dear reader – question my views, throw out whatever you disagree with me on, grab whatever is useful to you from these pages and use them to grow. We are all different and need different things at different times. Growth takes process and time.

Growing up I always hated the name I was given at birth. The incident with bully #3 only exacerbated it. I had problems just hearing the name as it carried the trauma within it in the sound waves. As I said earlier, I never told anyone about it when it happened. The first person I ever told was my husband. However during this time in my life my mother and I were going through our own process to forge a friendship based on choosing to be connected. This involved many discussions of past situations where our perspectives had caused us to act in a manner that hurt each other. We had never had talks like this before. We made ourselves vulnerable to each other. In this I shared my story of bully #3 and she was shocked and cut to the heart. She wept. Her compassion surprised me. I expected her to discount it. But then she went further. She suggested I change my name. Wow! Was she really suggesting that? I was shocked. That thought had never occurred to me. I had never seen it as mine to change. I don't know who I thought it belonged to. Perhaps I was too busy trying to internally separate from it. But owning my name. Wow. That was so deep to me I had to ponder it, pray.

After some time I made the decision to do it. Then came the process. How does one pick a name for themselves? **The Pursuer** turned this into a beautiful lesson. I have always had a fascination with names. I think it is because I understand how it effects the one hearing it said of them. I went through name books and imagined being called the various names and read what they meant. I had to "see" myself as the name I chose. And then I found it – Danielle, which means God is my judge. **The Pursuer** showed me how that position belongs to him alone. I have no business judging anyone, not even myself. He showed me where it says in the Bible *"Who* *art thou that judgest another man's servant? to his own master he standeth or falleth...* " It was true that I had been critical with others but I had been far more critical with myself and I was graciously being told to "stop it." So every time I hear my name now it is to remind me and there was no judgment in that either. Just that elegant grace. I had lived so much in opposition to myself like it talks about in the Bible (2 Timothy 2:25) God was giving me new thinking and the ability to acknowledge the truth.

Not everyone was happy about this name change though. For a year or so I had a family member refuse to comply with this change. They had been told by another person with religious authority in their eyes that I was in rebellion and dishonoring my parents. Strange because my one living parent suggested the change. My mother also told me that Danielle was the name that my father had originally chose but they changed their mind. And then there are those people in the Bible that God changed their name (Abram/ Abraham, Sarai/Sarah, Cephas/Peter, Saul/Paul, Isaac/Israel). So even though it was painful to endure that opposition **The Pursuer** had me internally strong enough that *the JAB!* had no access to harm. Yet I need more help than this name change. The internal lies, fears and traumas go deep. My mind was quite polluted by *the JAB!*. Confusion and condemnation would arise and I would get disoriented. To address this **The Pursuer** gave me His words to answer those accusing thoughts. I wrote them down in the specific order they were given. They interrupted the tendency to try to figure out the "who, what, when, where, why," of it all that would allow the negative process to continue.

This is a copy of what I wrote down:

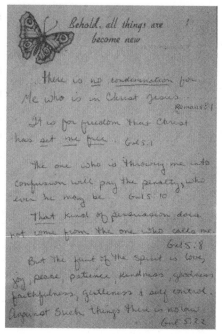

I use this for quite some time. I begin to see the love in the God who saved me. I love him so much for all he has done for me. I know I am not who I was before. I am healthy. My little family is amazing. We laugh, we play, we dance. I discover a lady minister named Joyce Meyer that I learn so much from. Having departed from certain legalistic things I heard the song *"True Colors"* recorded by Cyndi Lauper on the radio. It is the first "secular" music I've listened to for many years. It comes to me through the airwaves as if **The Pursuer** is singing the song to me himself validating my existence. I even buy the album. (mocking gasp) I had broken and discarded all non-Christian music I owned ten years earlier. It was a good thing at the time but I had definitely "thrown the baby out with the bathwater." *The JAB!* tries to steal this tender exchange through a certain lady in a leadership position at the new church we are a part of by warning me that this is not Christian music and how I shouldn't listen to it. Her admonishment brought fear and I considered "obeying" her words but **The Pursuer** gave me the strength to not let go. He was speaking life and comfort to my soul through it. With poetry and music **The Pursuer** goes deeper in writing love on my soul.

Revelation of Love

© Danielle Bernock 1988

Bound in myself – how do I get out
Trapped in my unbelief – how do I get out
Many years, many tears, prayers & crying out
Oh God I want to know you're there
And the truth is that you care
Why is it so hard?
Why do I believe you want to destroy me?
>   Honesty you used to break open the lock
>   Your love rescued me.

HONESTY

©Margaret Becker

Tonight by the glow
Of the firelight
You found the courage
To speak your mind
And tear down the walls
You've been hiding behind
You spoke of your struggle
And you cried from the pain
You spoke of your failure
And then you turned in shame
You said you knew you'd never
Be alright

Chorus
God's not afraid of your honesty

Emerging With Wings

He can heal your heart if you speak honestly
Humble sorrow and the honest cry
He will not pass by

So many of us
Spend so much time
Smoothing things over
Pretending we're fine
As if life could ever be
So cut and dried
But you my friend
You've got that passionate heart
It'll curse you sometimes
But it can take you far
When you let Him tame it
You will be just fine

Chorus

You may feel like you're crawling
Over broken glass
Crying a river
Into the pillows of your past
But you will be free

FOUND

Before I was known you knew me
Being unplanned I was planned
Before I followed you called me
You had my life in your hand

Why did you find me
Why did you search me out
Why do you love
Why don't you ever give up – on – me
        I tried to but…

In the darkest of darkest you were there
        In the loudest of noise I could hear – you

In the deepest of silence – I pained – I feared
        I ran – I cried
        "I don't understand" – and you heard.
        And you saw & you --- you understood

Precious yes precious in your sight
To be called precious is past all joy
In the eyes of my Father, my protector, my love, my redeemer
        I found, where I belong

---- I'm a twinkle in my father's eye

JUST COME IN

©Margaret Becker

What do I see
You draggin up here
Is that for your atoning?
I know you're sorry
I've seen your tears
You don't have to show Me
What makes you think you must
Make that go away

Emerging With Wings

I forgot
When I forgave
I wish you would

Chorus
Just come in
Just leave that right there
Love does not care

Just come in
Lay your heart right here
You should never fear

You think you've crossed
Some sacred line
And now I will ignore you
If you look up
You will find
My heart is still toward you
Look at the sky
The east to the west
That's where I threw this
When you first confessed
Let it go now

Chorus

I will forgive you
No matter what you've done
No matter how many times
You turn and run
I love you
I wish you'd come

I listen to this song over and over and over again endeavoring to believe not knowing what is in the way. But **The Pursuer** knows and so continues and continues.

I SEE

© Danielle Bernock 1990

I see behind your big blue eyes
the smile you hide your face behind
I see the sorrow of your heart
the pain you think I do not see
I know what's there & I do care.

Surrounded by such festivities
with pain welling up inside of me
Others not seeing, not knowing
what's happening in my heart

> But I do see, and I do care
> I do see, I've been there

Close those eyes & think of me
I'm closer than you see
Still your mind & still your heart
and reach for me, think of me
The pain so real within your heart
I understand, it once was mine

> I do see, and I do care
> I do see, I've been there

You see
I am a man of sorrow, acquainted with grief
People ran away, <u>my</u> people rejected me

But my father's will had to be done
I was obedient, I was lonely
My heart cried out for intimacy
My place with my Father,
Intimacy, that's what you want with me.

--

I do see, & I do care
I do see, I'll take you there

That last part? That came SEVEN years after the rest. It is staggering how long this process is taking. But I **am** making progress. I **am** thinking different. I **am** learning. I **am** growing. I'm even teaching some. I make a book for kids to use to spend time alone with God themselves with songs, scriptures and puzzles. I love spending time with God every day and teaching my kids. I think I'm doing really well. And I am, but also not. I intentionally choose to believe this God who saved me loves me. I even scream out loud "my God loves me" in the face of contrary circumstances screaming at me. This choice brings progress yet I still struggle with so much fear.

UNTITLED

© Danielle Bernock 1991

How could I be so foolish?
How could I not see?
There you were, all along
Talking & ministering to me.
My ears were deaf
My eyes were blind

The obvious I did not grasp
There you were, all along
Supplying what I need
Unstop my ears
Anoint my eyes
Fill me with yourself
Overflow me, overshadow me
Let it be you that others see

I see so clearly the danger
Of the trap I've encountered
Time & time again
So obscure, yet so clear
So strong is the fear
I will fall in the obvious snare

Only your grace, only your face
Only your being near me, inside me, around me
Surround me, protect me for you.

And oh how his grace covered us. We purchase our first home only to have my husband laid off *(JAB!)* the week after we sign papers but hadn't even moved in yet. And it was right before Christmas. I didn't do so well with that. Fear and worry. After we moved in my mother and mother in law came over to encourage us and brought a basket of goodies. The basket said on the side "let not your heart be troubled" and my rude response came bursting out in a voice of anguish "it's too late!" With that I marched out of the room and down to the basement to hide. But what happened next jolted me. As I marched down the stairs with my crappy attitude the voice of **The Pursuer** spoke to my heart so loudly I wondered if it was an audible voice. I don't think it was. But what he said to me was *"even your greatest fear cannot destroy you."* And with that **The Pursuer** addressed the fear of the fear, and condemnation due to the fear, spiral I had going on inside me. It didn't remove all anxiety from me but hope replaced a layer of the fear that I had accepted from the book of Job. Job laments that what he had greatly feared had come upon him (Job 3:25). That terrified me because I had so much fear in me. **The Pursuer** has plans to rid me of fear no matter how long it takes because he loves me. He speaks to my heart that he even plans to restore the years of loss (Joel 2:25). He started by providing for the replacement of my wedding ring. I had pawned my first one to pay bills. This second one was better and it was a visual for me to remember that promise of restoration. Soon after we moved in my husband got a better job that paid more than he ever had before.

The following year was both wonderful and terrible at the same time. Having learned some good and correct things about this God who loves me and then also learn some not correct things *(JAB!)* the results are mixed. I learn so much but don't understand what I think I'm supposed to understand. I get fearful and I calm down. I operate in some new "spiritual gifts" which is exhilarating. Yet my soul is not secure in the love of God so I seek approval and validation from people in authority. I learn some things about "rest" according to the Bible but don't really get it. My mother got diagnosed with cancer *(JAB!)* and I make a "prescription" for her of scriptures about healing to help her reach for life. We have teacher troubles *(JAB!)* at the school our kids are at and I have trouble addressing it *(JAB!)* which causes me to question my parenting but then I remind God the scriptures he had given me regarding them. For my mother's sixty fifth birthday my brother and I arrange her dream trip to Hershey Pennsylvania at Christmas time for her and I. I struggle with wanting to feel closer to God and don't really grasp the true meaning of Immanuel so I pray for God to be with us, when he already is. Back and forth, back and forth. **The Pursuer** encourages me over and over throughout the year and gives me this on the drive home from Hershey.

UNTITLED

© Danielle Bernock 1993

If only you knew, could grasp & could see
If only you understood, comprehended, perceived
The depth of my love for you
It goes beyond your abilities of sense
It goes beyond your thoughts & emotions
It is larger & deeper & further & more intense
The depth of my love for you

Oh my Lord - How can I know what is beyond me
How can I understand
How can I grasp or perceive
The depth of your love for man
If it is beyond my abilities
If it is further than all of my senses
Give me a revelation, a taste
Show me what you're telling me
But how oh how can I perceive
Give me of your anointing
I want to know
The depth of your love for me

7

❧And So…

The following year my mother died. It was such a bittersweet thing. I had never before gone through a death where I was personally convinced that the departed was with Jesus in heaven. I had hopes, wishes etc. but had never been certain before. In fact, after the God who loves me apprehended me I pressed him regarding all those previous deaths but mostly my brother. Especially because I had learned he had not indeed been murdered but rather died from something called auto erotic asphyxia. My mother had lied *(JAB!)* to me "to protect me." Yeah, it didn't work like that because lies cannot protect. I had never heard of auto erotic asphyxia and when I learned what it was my fears and earning mentality caused me to wonder if someone who had done that could be in heaven. I reeled back & forth inside. **The Pursuer** answered me. He did not answer my question but instead directed my attention to my focus. He spoke to my heart using words found in the Bible where Jesus was talking to Peter when Peter was preoccupied with what John was doing. *"What is that to thee? Follow thou me."* It was the wake up slap I needed. It was true. My focus on my dead brother was without any power. Where ever he was he was already and all my lamenting in the world wouldn't change anything. If he was in hell did I want to go there? Where was I with all this? Instead of on him, my focus needed to be on me, I still have a life, what am I going to do with it? Who am I going to follow? Choice. I chose God even though I didn't understand. So the peace and comfort I had concerning my mother helped a great deal in the face of the unimaginable pain of the loss. My mother and I had not been close growing up, in fact quite the contrary, but our journey to become friends melded us together. Even though I wanted more, I rejoiced that she had received what she reached for with her faith and love for God. She had asked for one more of every holiday. She lived fourteen months which exceeded her diagnosis of six months or less. I was so grateful to have shared that time with her, been privileged to serve her, walk with her through her journey. **The Pursuer** gave me my final request with my mother which was to be with her when she passed. I held her hand and sang to her. She even waved goodbye to me and I told her it was not good bye because I would see her again later. Grieved to the core yet I had no regrets. Bittersweet.

Processing grief, seeing yourself an orphan and cleaning out your childhood home is no small emotional task. I was so thankful for the hospice grief program that helped me. This is also where I learned about compound losses *(JAB!)* and how toxic unresolved grief is *(JAB!)*. I had a lot of that unresolved stuff resurface *(JAB!)*. This information helped me not only process my mother's death successfully but also validate and begin addressing all those multiple losses and traumas from earlier in my life that had gone septic underground.

Following the settling of my mother's affairs we took the opportunity to move due to an inheritance my mother had left us. We moved to an older house that had lots of "potential" which made it affordable. Still it was one of those "step of faith" things. It was ginormous! Three thousand four hundred and forty two square feet with five bedrooms and three full bathrooms. It had a built in pool and huge yard. We thought it was our piece of heaven. It was in many ways even though at times it seemed a money pit. It was here that I heard **The Pursuer** speak to me again. Quite unexpectedly. That quiet voice inside. I still remember where I was standing. He identified some things in my mother's life that had made her ill and let me know that I needed to address them in my life if I wanted to change the direction in my life - to live. The primary thing being I needed to stop numbing out my feelings. During our trip to Hershey my mother had a good cry and we shared an intense time of belly laughter that brought her to tears. My mother told me she had not done either of those for years due to burying her feelings. **The Pursuer** was shining light on this to save me from destroying myself. Between the severity of the soul pain I had felt and being told repetitively "you're too emotional"/"too sensitive" I erroneously believed that my feelings were bad. Whenever I thought that what I felt about anything was "unacceptable" I drove it underground with disallowance picking up what I was "supposed to feel" like a "good child" (using words from my new counselor). And so I began. And with that information added to the help I received from the hospice grief program eventually I formulated my own program and began offering it to help others. One of the scientific things I learned from grief recovery is that grief tears are good. Grief tears are healing. Tears of grief carry a toxic enzyme out of the body. **The Pursuer** invented science so he already knew that. He also knew better than I that thing called "process."

Part of this process was a particular year/year and half following a ladies retreat I went on where we were all given "a word from the Lord" (personal prophecy) from a particular person who was said to have this gift. I was skeptical. Especially because what I was initially given seemed too convenient. I was clearly still grieving the loss of my mother and the scripture I was given was Psalm 147:3 about God healing the broken hearted. Like I said, convenient. But then in the "word" I was given I was told that God would do it (heal my broken heart) and that I didn't need to be uncomfortable with who I am because God had created me specifically. That second part pierced me deeply as only the God who loved me knew the deep extent I was uncomfortable in my own skin. **The Pursuer** immediately went into action and confirmed the words of healing in my heart. I was stunned as he elaborated that not only the pain from the loss of my mother but he was going to heal the brokenness of my entire life. I could not have made that up because it was beyond my grasp. Yet every day for that season, I "felt" him with me. Every day I would sit on the floor and listen with headphones on to the same three songs from a Winds of Worship recording that He directed me to. Deep wailing & weeping came out as love and hope washed over my soul. His presence with me would surprise me as we would have conversations like I never had before. It was unexpected. It was euphoric. One particular "conversation" we had was regarding what happened to me at that church when I was a child. **The Pursuer** reminded me of something Jesus had said about a millstone and a child. He said that applied to me and that he held that pastor accountable. I burst into tears as I didn't really understand what he meant by accountable *(JAB!)* and I had just recently learned that pastor had hung himself. I felt responsible *(JAB!)* but I knew I had forgiven him. My husband and I went to that church prior to our wedding as a demonstration of that forgiveness. Confused I couldn't receive any more insight but was able to receive the comfort that it was not my fault this pastor did what he did. That was just one of many layers and the first time **The Pursuer** "touched" the bull's-eye I didn't know existed. He was not at all surprised at my recoil.

The next many years are filled with much learning and growth. Much laughter. Much tears. More intimate times with **The Pursuer** bringing more healing. I feel like this is where in the movies they play that scene change music and pan through the seasons. Our little family of four, we go on vacations, play games together, go on mission trips and have parties. We had as many parties as we could. We all become very involved in various ministries at the church we called home. I even headed up one called Adopt-A-Teen where adults are paired with teenagers to pray for them and encourage them. Something that I wish I would have had available to me growing up. Through all of this **The Pursuer** continues relentlessly and repetitively teaching me, wasting nothing but turning everything into lessons to convince me of his love and remove the layers of pain. Over and over and over and over. Times of teaching through sermons, books, teaching tapes, seminars, prophecies, dreams, music, movies and just every day stuff. Times of letting it soak in – just living life, loving and enjoying my little family and applying the things taught as best as possible. Making progress. Even so I struggled with that perception of being excluded and just could not understand how to overcome it. I attempt to seek counsel with people who I see as included but I find no answers. I even put myself out there and ask to be included by "them" but am told no. Rejected at that place called church *again*. I work harder. In the process of my voracious appetite to grow I become well versed in what some people call "Christianese" *(JAB!)*.

This timeframe of my life I find it very difficult to address. So much so that I wrestle with just stopping *(JAB!)*, hearing "who do I think I am that anyone would want to read about my story" play in my head *(JAB!)*. I ponder if Joyce Meyer had similar thoughts. She is my primary role model of both the courage to share and the value of being vulnerable.

Today I went to lunch with my friend Amy and she echoed my difficulty with these years. She knew me back then. She spoke of how it was apparent to her that **The Pursuer** was there. How she thought I always seemed happy and she was somewhat puzzled over what I was going through, addressing, had uncovered etc... I said yeah, I know, that is my challenge. That is all true, but... word fail. I tell her I even talked with my counselor about it today. There is SO much good it is too tedious to cover. There are negative things with names attached that I have no desire to slander. I struggle with what is important because it is ALL important.

Hmm that reminds me of a quote I recently came across by the author of a book called *"The Shack."* I haven't read it. I was warned by various sources that it was dangerous. I don't remember the specifics any longer but it had that vague *"lead me into darkness" (JAB!)* thing that still hid in the back of my mind (fear). So I heeded the warnings. Listened to "the authority" I perceived they carried over me – like a "good child" (there is my new counselor again). Even though a good friend of mine chose it as a book to study with a group of ladies I gathered with each month. One of which was Amy who I had lunch with today. Again Hmm. That happened during this difficult to elaborate on time frame. There were other situations similar to this coming from various sources. Warnings. Restrictions. Conditions. They attached like invisible burrs to the plethora of lessons from **The Pursuer.** The unsaid *"if you want to belong you better..."* That *"aww you better not, tsk tsk*

tsk" voice of threatening in my head *(JAB!)*. Things I should be doing. Things I needed to do before I was allowed to do what I desired (earning). So I'd take my assigned place like a "good child" (there she is again). Because of that, certain things **The Pursuer** brought into my life "they" *(JAB!)* successfully impeded. But then I'd be confused by things "they" did that I thought were "bad" *(JAB!)*. Yet during this entire time frame **The Pursuer** was clearly there teaching me, speaking to me and even speaking through me. His grace is freaking amazing. He wasted no opportunity. Used every resource I was capable of tapping into no matter its source. In fact *"The Matrix"* was one of the movies I initially didn't watch due to some warning but later did watch at the encouragement of my son. **The Pursuer** watched it with me & taught me many things. This both delighted and puzzled me.

Real Life

© Danielle Bernock 2001

I want to live in the realm
of the real.
O God I cry out
Save me from religion.
Outward show
with no inward change.
That evil place of deception.

Help me keep fresh
my childlike faith.
The wonder and awe of you.
To follow each day
in an old and new way,
what you have shown and do show.

Help me to live in the realm of the real.
The way, the truth, the life.

It is just simply amazing to look back and see how **The Pursuer** was never swayed by my foolish behavior and double minded ups and downs – even though I was taught that with those issues I should not think I would receive *"anything" (JAB!)* from the Lord (James 1:7) and so I would fear because I saw that no matter how hard I tried I fell short. And I would try so hard I would literally hurt myself. And then I'd be told I try too hard and I'm too hard on myself and I didn't know what to do with that. Another trap. But **The Pursuer** knew my heart. And just like he knew the heart of the pagan king Abimelech (Genesis 20:6) and responded with grace instead of judgment, grace is what **The Pursuer** poured on me in the face of multiple failures. Relentless to set me free, step by step, layer by layer. Through my children's upbringing and my mistakes as a parent. Through bad decisions and the resulting consequences. Through empty nest and moving across the country. Through isolation and depression and digging to the root.

YOU ARE MY GRACE

© Danielle Bernock 8/21/2009

Source of all life you know my heart
You hear it singing as I write
Of how I long to do your will
And feel that satisfaction of your pleasure
Your Spirit whispers, your Word speaks and I make my choice
I choose you, I choose you
So I run full speed ahead to follow your voice
Expectation of joy, expectation of joy

And So...

Source of all love you know my heart
Your hear it weeping as I write
You understand, you understand
That when I arrive at a place you call there
And unexpectedly find grief and despair
You are my Grace, you are my Grace

Almighty Agape, Everlasting Holiness
Incorruptible Righteousness, Undaunted Mercy
Faithful Intercessor, Graceful Redeemer
I thank you, I thank you
You are my Grace, you are my Grace

My Grace in the face of discouragement
My Grace in the face of pain
My Grace that teaches me how to breathe
When dreams turn to dust and the pain overwhelms
My Grace when your people disappoint
My Grace when I am just like them
My Grace to face what lies ahead
In the dark, where I cannot see
But you can, for you are Light

My Grace to respond to pat answers
My Grace to false accusations
My grace when I fail, My Grace when I prevail
My Grace to climb these mountains
Be they in life, or in my soul
You are my Grace, You are sufficient
You are my Grace, You are sufficient
I will come forth
Either walking or standing, Or you carrying me

Emerging With Wings

I will come forth
For YOU are my Grace

8

❧ To the Core or so I Thought ❧

Just as the lies, pains and traumas were built one on another likewise they needed to be "un" built. I had no idea how complex and pervasive the damage was to my soul so I often became critical *(JAB!)* and impatient with myself. That did not help. **The Pursuer** gently continued.

One layer in "un" building occurred when the God who loved me walked me through the following lesson. It was extremely difficult for me to follow his instructions. It caused excruciating inner pain and I wept as I obeyed. I know there are those who will respond with "I wish God would tell me to do that." I have encountered some already. It was obvious to me they had no understanding of what really was going on and also had no need of the lesson I had been given. I needed it deep, irremovable, engraved on my soul. He was successful.

What was this lesson? I will call it a "closet cleanse." It was a demonstrative lesson regarding my value. He had me go through ALL of my clothes and get rid of ALL of them that had not been acquired new. I could only keep them if they were purchased new or were a gift. ALL hand me downs, ALL thrift store and garage sale purchases had to be removed. That is where some jump in and say "How in the world could that be difficult? I want a new wardrobe! I wish God would have ME do that!!" To you I say "you do not understand." All was all. That included sentimental things. That included irreplaceable things – like some items I held onto from my mother that had died. I had favorites that I had to get rid of. With each one I had to pry a piece of my heart off of, like prying open a hand gripping something for dear life. The lesson was for me to make room for the idea that I am of great value – far above second hand. This was a removal not an addition. He walked me through a visual demonstration to remove the second hand opinion of myself. There was no part that addressed the replacement of clothing at this time. I understood that was not the issue and somehow was not concerned. I knew it was the beginning of the lesson and adding would come after. I still didn't know how to internalize the great value thing but it was definitely a step in that direction.

Getting to the core required more change in my thinking, my perspectives and my understanding. To enlarge my view **The Pursuer** took some drastic measures. Taking opportunity of my husband's recent job loss we were directed to move across the country from Michigan to Arizona via a new job. This changed everything. Changed my home, my job, my climate, my time zone, my peer group, my grocery stores, pizza places and the list goes on. It was what I didn't know I needed.

We were empty nesters so one might think it was perfect timing. However the move was devastating to the dreams I held and the life I had been building. Both our children were newly married and my dreams of family get togethers and grandchildren danced in my head. Sometimes the feelings played like it was the end of the world. Yet the God who loved me made it clear that it was his plan and since he was the one who started this whole thing (been in that place before) I had a peace and a sense of adventure (that faith thing) that cohabitated with horrific pain (fear of loss and lack of vision). That was a most bizarre feeling and I didn't understand how to deal with it. Although I mentally required myself to be fine (*JAB!*) my body rebelled with panic attacks (*JAB!*) less than a month after my husband went ahead to take the job. That basket case you read about earlier in this story visibly bobbed up and down as on good days or moments I was able to apply things I had learned but on bad days or moments issues I had not identified yet internally gripped me (*JAB!*). My daughter came along side me and entered my pain.

Because the job began in November I stayed behind to allow us to celebrate Christmas before packing up and selling the house. Music was a great salve for my soul and I applied it liberally and often. I had an old social media site back then and someone I didn't know put the song *"Brave"* by Gavin Mikhail on my page. I had never heard of it or him. I credit **The Pursuer** because this song played in my heart like the God who loved me and I were singing it to each other. It provided the courage I needed. I clung to it as my personal life preserver. It validated instead of ignoring the fear without giving it the permission to have control while intentionally engaging trust. That faith thing.

That song stayed with me for quite a while and the God who loved me provided more. *"Landslide"* (Seven Places), *"Keep Holding On"* (Avril Lavigne), *"Let Me Take You There"* (Plain White Ts), *"Save Me"* (7 Sharp 9), *"Nothing But the Blood"*

(The Swift) and *"Stand in the Rain"* (Superchick).

After the move the peace side of the feeling battle in me got stronger yet the conflict remained. I didn't understand. It seemed odd. It amazed me when I came across a song that embodied that internal conflict of feelings and elaborated on buried feelings. A song called *"Whatever You're Doing (Something Heavenly)"* by Sanctus Real carried **The Pursuer's** fingerprints.

And yes he was up to something bigger than I imagined. He was methodically making his way to the core. We rented a lovely home next to South Mountain. But it was farther away from my husband's work than we wanted and on what I called the back side of a mountain because I felt banished like Moses after he killed an Egyptian in the book of Genesis.

> It amazed me when I came across a song that embodied that internal conflict of feelings and elaborated on buried feelings. The lyrics to *"Whatever You're Doing (Something Heavenly)"* by Sanctus Real that carried **The Pursuer's** fingerprints are provided in this QR code.

I knew I was not actually banished but we were indeed isolated. We just "knew" it was intentional even though we didn't understand. Now I can compare it to a butterfly inside the cocoon. We were set in a place for privacy and growth. I have learned that when a caterpillar is in the cocoon that it partially digests itself in the transformation process. I can see that parallel too as I recall some not so pretty times during this transforming process.

I had moved ten times before and this was the first time I did not completely unpack. After our one year lease was up we were going to buy a house but **The Pursuer** stepped in and saved us from making that mistake which kept us from becoming a statistic in the economic downturn that devastated many home owners in 2008. We were very grateful for that protection that made us feel loved but very confused when my husband was laid off *(JAB!)* from the job that moved us there as well as subsequent employment issues we encountered.

When Moses was living out in the desert he had banished himself. It was not God who did that. In fact **The Pursuer** came and found him, hence the story of the burning bush. Likewise us, two years later we were struggling with depression *(JAB!)* and it was intensified by our coming thirty year anniversary because we had no way to celebrate. **The Pursuer** stepped in again. We got an email that seemed too good to be true so of course we were skeptical. But it said it was from a ministry that we knew and are partners with so we didn't delete it. Instead my husband called to verify and to our shock and amazement it was true. This ginormous international ministry was inviting <u>US</u> to a weekend called "Behind the Mission," where we would have personal contact with them, they were going to pay for our room in the nice hotel, a visit to the spa (complete with massage) and feed us. Plus it was over our anniversary weekend! Wow!

That weekend changed our lives. The God who loves us took notice of us when we had felt invisible. We saw in action things we had read about. We were provided (free of charge) tools specific to what we needed and had wonderful inspiring conversations that evidenced **The Pursuer.** One of the books I was given *"Protecting Your Family in Dangerous Times"* provided instruction on a tool **The Pursuer** had tried to provide for me previously (something called pleading the blood) but I dropped it *(JAB!)* due to listening to someone I had given spiritual authority to in my life. They had called it unscriptural so those old fears *(JAB!)* led me to listen to them. **The Pursuer** without any condemnation showed me how he had found a way through music to insert the importance of the blood of Jesus in spite of my ignorant disregard. Grace. But perhaps the biggest take away was coming to see and believe that it was actually possible to live free from fear – something that had been a mirage. So we began that journey devouring the resources given. We learned that the spirit of fear is not attempting to simply scare us but to get us to not believe what **The Pursuer** (LOVE) has said.

Not too many months later the incident occurred. **The Pursuer** had already restored a measure of music back in my life in a somewhat unconventional way and put me in a place I said I never wanted to be. He used my weakness for authority as the pastor turned around one day, pointed in my face and commanded me to tell the worship leader that he said I needed to be on the worship team. My insides responded with that internal *"yes sir" (JAB!)*. So, I was singing on the worship team at the church we called home. I loved to worship but didn't want to perform. This team was different. One particular Sunday we were doing our usual practice and the sound/video guy was doing his usual set up of where we need to be standing and such. I do not stand still when I worship so he teasingly taped my feet to the stage and my co-singer burst out in hilarious laughter but my soul was pierced to the core *(JAB!)*. My reaction was visible. I did my best to control myself as they asked what was wrong and I couldn't answer but put on my business self as my mind raced and flashes of the past played in full emotion. After practice I went to the bathroom and had an absolute meltdown as the trauma of first grade repeatedly played in my soul. At the same time another part of me was trying to figure out what the heck was going on here. I was past that I thought. Here I am again. Someone on the team comforted me and prayed with me and I emerged from the bathroom making a different choice than I would have done before.

Previously I would have slinked out of the room, hidden in shame, and even gone home. I had done that before. This time I came out and talked with people. I apologized to the guy who was just trying to have fun. I felt so bad I made him feel so bad. He had no clue, he was just playing. Dave, the worship leader who is also a dear friend, gave me all grace and it was indeed amazing. He inquired if I was up to singing or if I wanted to opt out. It was a free choice. I made the choice to sing even though one of the songs was going to touch "that spot" with certain words. I took courage. It went well.

After this happened I talked to the God who loved me, prayed about it. I was tired of feeling ambushed by sudden emotional devastation *(JAB!)*, feeling powerless to overcome or stop it *(JAB!)*, finally recovering and feeling everything is ok until the cycle repeats *(JAB!)*. He reminded me of a previous time when we were going through a specific situation regarding one of our children. We would "stand on the Word" (read and speak promises from the Bible) but still we would encounter emotional moments that would incite our mouths to react negatively and we had learned that what we say is important. So to help us he gave us what I called "instead words." A specific short verbal response to say "instead" of what the emotions or fear wanted to say. This was very helpful as we practiced it and exercised power over our mouths in the heat of the moment. I named this a "silver bullet." Its purpose is to stop the emotions from gaining control of the mind with racing thoughts that come out in negative words fueled by fear. In short stop the attack dead in its tracks. It must be short. It must be specific. It must be backed by the Spirit of God carrying His power – truth. So I prayed for a silver bullet for this. But first I needed to find the root. What am I even addressing?? I didn't know and that was part of the problem. I needed to examine: When the attack *(JAB!)* occurs, where does it "dump" me off? What is it attempting to accomplish? What is the lie I have believed? So I sat down and **The Pursuer** ushered me through the toxic lie sequence that would present itself more in emotion than words, to the truth that would quench it.

I learned this silent progression (mindset) had been operating my <u>entire life</u> (entire life being a revelation – that was how it had such deep roots). This progression was involuntary and took place in a split second without conscious knowledge. It went something like this:

Just shut up, no one wants to hear what you have to say. You do not matter. Everyone else is more important than you. Run away before it shows and everyone sees. Shut up – you have nothing of value to say or be. Voice of the silenced.

The TRUTH – the above progression is a lie!

God gave me a message

God gave me a purpose

God gave me life

God favors me in Christ

The righteous are as bold as a lion

Stand on the Word

Speak the Word

I have value

I MATTER

Who am I? I am in process and that is ok. I am ok.

The silver bullet?

I MATTER!

Two words. This is a major breakthrough. Both the unveiling of the lie and the new weapon I have to use. As I practiced saying this out loud **The Pursuer** built a stronger and stronger perception of my value in my soul. He brought more input in my life to support that. Words. Sermons speaking of seeing myself as God sees me and what he saw was awesome. A poem elevating and validating my value as well as approving my humanity. It celebrated uniqueness and removed pressure to perform.

At this same time my best friend Christy is going through "incidents" herself and is in need of her own silver bullet. **The Pursuer** takes her through her own process because we all are irreplaceable creations of his love in need of a distinctive touch that is ours alone. She emerged from her process with **"What other people think is THEIR decision."** At the time I didn't understand it but that was irrelevant because it was hers not mine and it was perfect for her. But as time went by we shared them both for different reasons. Again **The Pursuer** tailoring answers to our needs. Every one of us matters to him. There is just one you. There is just one me. Just look at your hands – no one else has your fingerprints. You matter!

While watching a season of one of those talent shows on TV I noticed a particular contestant who ended up the winner. He carried such a "cool" demeanor that really impressed me. This led me to explore what I called "the secret of cool people." What makes "cool" people actually "cool?" I had previously had the mentality that they mattered more than the "uncool" or at least thought they did and bullied others into agreeing. But this young man didn't carry that arrogance. I identified a comfortableness he had with himself. They were "comfortable in their own skin." Something I had never been. I began to declare that out loud about myself – that I was comfortable in my own skin. It sounded funny but I did it anyways because that was what I wanted to be. It was no abracadabra but it began to change how I thought. That is what I have now learned is the real meaning of repentance – to think differently. Not the religious perception presented by many: to grovel *(JAB!)*, apologize, promise better behavior, work harder *(JAB!)*, feel remorse, adhere to certain rules or a moral code – no it was to discover how **The Pursuer** thinks and change my mind to think like Him. See the good He sees. It's not as easy as it might sound. Mindsets are called that because they are "set" or established thought patterns. These have been set through various means. It can be through misunderstanding the information, repetition, conditioning or just a single trauma. To un-set them takes various types of effort. It takes more than just being told we need to think differently. We need to learn how. It takes time. There is much discovery involved and it is more difficult for some than for others. Plus there is grace for the process.

Remember your fingerprints? Your story and your soul are just as unique. But we have overlaps. We effect each other so that gives us the power to help each other. Not everything helps everyone but everyone has something to offer to help. For example I came across something my friend Heather had posted on her social media site during this stage in my story. It was a quote I had never heard and spoke about how God and love are both not visible to our eyes but that doesn't mean they are absent. It resonated in me so I wrote it down and have read it out loud to myself daily since. It has changed a part of my mindset. It changed my definition of a word I had stuck in Christmas – Immanuel – God WITH me, even if I don't see or feel it. Another friend gave me a CD of teachings on the love of God. On one of these I learned a new term and a new vantage point was opened to me as he unveiled a condition he saw in people.

He called it "Christian dyslexia." I saw this condition in myself so I sought to understand and make changes. We had a guest speaker I had never heard of come and do a special series at our church that revolutionized my view of Grace. I bought the CD set and listened to them over and over and over. One of the ministries we partner with kept saying that God loves me as much as he loves Jesus but instead of helping me that confused me. Apparently I hadn't thought that much about that Father part of the thing called the trinity loving the Son part. I had it stuck in the death part. At a gathering in the home of our friends Nick and Kathy we watched a DVD series by a minister where he tied imagination to my thinking in a useful way. He talked about how we play movies in our minds with information in our lives. These movies can be worry filled or hope filled and we have the power to change the channel. I see it as setting presets by identifying what I choose to be focused on and intentionally programing it into myself by repetition – reading, speaking, watching, listening etc. Then when I come to a crisis or emotional situation my heart can retrieve what I have already put there. For example I had it suggested for me to read John chapters fourteen to seventeen in the Bible for twenty one consecutive days and I decided it was a good idea. I read them out loud in various translations which was cool. During this time I had the opportunity to re-watch *"The Passion"* movie. **The Pursuer** joined those two things in my perception showing me things I never knew before – revelation. Things I had read I "saw" in the movie. I obtained vision to become, instead of pressure to perform. All these pieces from different sources.

Even though some of the sources were "not my flavor" I rehearsed the information I gleaned from them anyways. I learned that term from another minister friend many years prior and it has helped me over and over to glean what does work or omit what does not work for me even without feeling like I'm saying they are bad. Not everyone likes apples or plums or carrots etc. but that does not make them bad. Like I said – not everything helps everyone but everyone has something to offer to help. Sometimes the lyrics to a song are good but we can't stand the tune. Maybe someone's tone of voice is difficult to listen to. I have read a book and wrote down one nugget of useful information and then thrown out the book still believing it was worth it to read it. I have books that have helped me in the past where I used to be but are no longer useful. We change and nobody is right all the time. We will find error in everything. We just need the right guide WITH us to show us what is for and not for us and the timing. **The Pursuer** is well able.

9

⊗ The Bull's-eye ⊗

Have you ever had a weird issue with your car that you had a ridiculous time getting fixed? You know, one of those things that it happens sometimes but not all the time. It fails to happen when you take it to the shop for repair. Or they notice it at the shop too but what they do to "fix" it doesn't work. Maybe you needed the part or work they did and maybe you didn't but it didn't fix the problem you came in for. Then you finally relent and take the car to the dealer because they should be the experts seeing "they made the car." This is true only to a point, because the auto company made the vehicle, not the mechanic. And then perhaps you've taken your car to one dealer only to be ripped off and the car is still not repaired. Perhaps it is better in some ways but worse in others, with the reason you brought your car in not being taken care of. So you don't want to go to another dealer. However your problem persists. So after much frustration you do some research or request referrals from trusted sources, relent and go to another dealer or a specialized mechanic who is supposed to know your vehicle. And Shazam! Your problem is identified and fixed.

I am seeing a parallel here with issues in life. We encounter various problems in our lives that we don't seem to be able to fix. Perhaps we know where they came from or maybe they arise seemingly out of nowhere. Whatever their origin, sometimes we can address them over and over but yet they persist. So we finally seek some help from friends' or counseling or books or what not and it helps but it doesn't "fix" the problem. At least not permanently. Then we finally relent and go to a church because they should be the experts on life. Some do find solutions but others are met with disappointment or worse. Some may find help in a few ways but then other things are made worse AND you are still left with the original problem you came with. So you say you'll never go to church again. They don't know what they are talking about. They are a bunch of hypocrites etc. However, your problem persists. So you do some research, seek referrals from people that seem to have what you long for so much and you are told of the real "dealer" (our creator God) and his "specialized mechanic" (Jesus who is the Word). This is where the answers to life are found – in "Christ" Jesus.

That "Christ" part? That is **The Pursuer.** That is the one who is WITH us – always. I learned this in a new light since our return to Michigan. It is what prompted me to begin this book, share my story. I am in such awe of the elegance and pervasiveness of His grace. How He never left me even when I felt so all alone. He was there when I sat on the floor of my closet in Arizona consumed with pain and seriously considered walking out into the middle of Baseline Road hoping to be crushed by a semi. He was there when I got that separating phone call that smashed my heart into a million pieces bringing inconceivable confusion and anguish. He was there when from my bed I heard a slam and my dad laid on the bathroom floor making those horrid noises and my mother went manic and time stood still. He was there when I was a teenager standing at the counter in the kitchen holding the bottle of pills contemplating taking them all just to make the pain stop. He was there when my dad was there but still not there He was there when that bully screamed lies in my face that I believed to be true. He was there when the bull's-eye occurred...

The definition of a bull's-eye is the center of any target and what we call any shot that hits that center. It is also attaining the highest achievement or success in something.

Have you ever asked yourself why do paper cuts and needle pokes hurt so intensely when a much "larger" wound feels smaller? The injury doesn't seem to justify the pain. The short and extremely over simplified answer is in the nerves. Here is a long and complicated answer that makes my head spin. There are things called "nociceptors" or nerve fibers in our bodies that send the touch/pain messages to a certain place in our brain. A place called the somatosensory cortex. This cortex thing processes information from all the systems in our bodies that are perceptive to touch. I thought touch was just a single sense, but it is actually many diverse sensory experiences working together. They are sensitivity to: pain, temperature, and a thing called the proprioception system (the body's perception of itself that oversees it's place in space). Head spinning yet? This whole system is extremely sophisticated and highly sensitive, that allows people to perceive and interpret a broad assortment of feelings or sensations. The network of nerve cells is across the whole body and ready to react when we experience the sensations related to our body's perception. These specialized cells react as they were designed by our creator. Some react to pain, but others respond to passing breezes, the heat of the sun, draft from a window, pressure etc. The stimuli travel along these nerves through this complex system to the thalamus first which then passes the information on to the cortex. In experience – the injury hits a small bull's-eye regarding skin pain. It looks like such a small thing that we have difficulty validating the pain. But it is not the size of the injury, it is where it occurred and what it affected. Simply amazing, these bodies our creator designed!

I took a concealed pistol license class where in my instructor took great pains to inform us that if we went forward with the decision to carry a weapon we had better be prepared to kill a human being. I found his approach appalling. He was far more extreme than was necessary and wielded fear with great skill *(JAB!)*. His aim was to pass only "serious" people. His tactic worked on me – I chose to pass on getting my CPL as I had no interest in training myself into a killer. I only wanted to shoot targets and definitely was not a serious student by his measure. However much to my surprise **The Pursuer** used this class. That in and of itself is amazing to me. He loves us so very much that he will use whatever is available to help us. His challenge so often is that He has so little available to Him, or we are not paying attention. But I am getting off point here.

In this class I learned some very valuable information about what a bull's-eye is and how to achieve one. We were required to watch the shootout scene of a movie called *"In the Line of Duty"* about real criminals named Platt and Matix who robbed a bank in 1986. This historic incident lasted less than five minutes yet approximately one hundred forty five shots were

This historic incident lasted less than five minutes yet approximately one hundred forty five shots were exchanged. More details of this incident are provided in the QR code.

exchanged. Our instructor went on to elaborate on which person used which gun and narrated the scene pointing out success and failure. Who lived, who died and why. The guns the FBI used failed them so badly in this confrontation that they threw them away. Our instructor told us that the caliber of a gun is irrelevant and contrary to popular belief it is not the hole that kills. It is the shock wave (the transfer of energy) that damages. He went on to tell us how resilient humans are and what is needed to be able to stop one. Having the proper weapon and proper ammunition are important. The proper training that breeds consistency, accuracy and steadiness under stress are much more important. But knowing where to aim it all – the bull's-eye – THAT is where you get the highest achievement or success. In a human body there are only two places in which to achieve this.

So by now perhaps you are wondering what in the world does this have to do with anything in this book. It is key. It is what unlocked the revelation of the cause of years of suffering in my life. As you have read earlier in this book of the accumulative traumas that individually may seem small (perhaps like paper cuts) but put together caused much injury. But even handicapped I kept going. That is loosely compared to Platt in the movie who was shot twelve times before he acquired the necessary damage and he died. None of the twelve singularly hit either of the two places to obtain the bull's-eye success.

While writing this book **The Pursuer** safely ushered me to the place where He unveiled a bull's-eye lie that the enemy of our souls *(the JAB!)* had so silently placed in my tender and vulnerable child heart. How it succeeded I did not understand at the time but as **The Pursuer** revealed it I gasped as the truth was so clear and I saw how it had touched virtually every area of my life in some way from that point on. He *(the JAB!)* had previously and consistently hit that same spot to prepare it for this hit. *"you don't belong in your family – they never wanted you" "God is dangerous" "authorities have the power" "you deserve excessive punishment" "you have no power or voice" "you have no value" "you don't deserve to breathe" "God does not care" "not good enough and never will be" "perfection required" "never to be accepted" and on* **that** day *"you don't matter" "Pastor's don't have time for you" "how could you be so stupid?" "why are you wasting our time?" "what is wrong with you anyways?"* … and with the shock wave of absolute exclusion, the transfer of energy plummeted my soul into an abyss of despair sitting on the front row of that church, cast out and bereft*, the inception of the lie silently took place. The twisted perversion of a scripture without using words. The opposite of truth became a hidden part of my every expectation. *The JAB!* inverted the very words of Jesus that said in John 6:37, *"All that the Father giveth me shall come to me; and him that cometh to me I will in no wise cast out."* In my heart I had come to Jesus and was cast out by those I saw as Jesus, meaning I believed Jesus himself had cast me out. He didn't want me anymore than my family did. Spiritually orphaned.

These religious leaders offered me a way to earn what should have been given. They required me to prove myself worthy. These instructions in self effort to overcome the inversion created a vicious circle that I stayed trapped in for many years. An invisible cage. I came to Jesus at that tender age and I was "cast out" as not good enough by the authorities I believed held all the power and then instructed in earning acceptance. It left a deep expectation of being cast out wherever I went with the only hope being if I worked hard enough I might gain some sort of acceptance, or more accurately put – tolerance. The exclusion was absolute. I had no real expectation that anyone at any time would ever truly love me. How **The Pursuer** unveiled this exposed the heinous lie. And I saw **The Pursuer** who wooed me with that song on those poster boards. I saw how He had been pursuing me ever since – because it is true that I came to Him and He *"will in NO WISE"* (not in any way) cast me out – I am forever accepted in the beloved, made righteous by Himself, eternally loved and forgiven, NEVER to be separated from His love.

Now begs the question. How could God have let this happen? I was just a child. I do not have all the answers but I have some insight. As I said, **The Pursuer** was there – but his hands were tied. He had not "orphaned" me as the wounding in my soul believed *(JAB!)*. Where this occurred may have been "a church" but it was one where darkness had been given access. Given a place. I believe **The Pursuer** is the Holy Spirit and this group of people had acted against Him. They had voted out the light He had sent them and in the absence of light darkness prevails. Jesus warned when light is dark – how great is that darkness. (Matt 6:23 / Luke 12:35) Lies flourish in darkness and lies alienated my young heart *(JAB!)*. I had no human there to protect me *(JAB!)*. **The Pursuer** found no one to "stand in the gap" for me like it talks about in the Bible. The lies had been built at home first *(JAB!)*.

For years all of this was buried, discounted like a single paper cut when it was more like thousands. I couldn't validate it in my mind *(JAB!)*, constantly comparing my "small" problem to large traumas like tsunamis and plane crashes. But like a beach ball pushed under water will resurface so the pain and lie recycled in my life *(JAB!)*. I would do very well for long periods of time and then suddenly and unexpectedly an eruption of that despair of disconnection *(JAB!)*. Bereft*. **The Pursuer** even spoke to these things with words of affirmation, comfort yet it wasn't deep enough. He had to expose the root before he was able to gently reveal this bull's-eye freeing me with the truth of His unconditional LOVE. Light is good but to those who have been in the dark for a long time too much light too soon is painful. **The Pursuer** is kind, gentle and patient.

*Bereft https://www.vocabulary.com/dictionary/bereft
So, they took the thing you most loved, and you're never going to get it back. You've gone beyond just plain grief-stricken —
you're *bereft*.
sorrowful through loss or deprivation
Synonyms: bereaved, grief-stricken, grieving, mourning, sorrowing, sorrowful
experiencing or marked by or expressing sorrow especially that associated with irreparable loss
unhappy in love; suffering from unrequited love
Synonyms: lovelorn, unbeloved, unloved, not loved

10

〰〰〰 The ARGHHHH!

ARGGGGGGGHHHHHH!

So here I am again. Stuck in that frustration. So much to say. So many details. What the freak is important? It all is – to me. But this book isn't for me. It's to share, to help, to encourage, to shine a light into a darkness that hides in shame pretending it isn't there or perhaps pretends to be light. The work in my heart so elegant, so specific, so vast – so personal. The life, the freedom, the joy I have come to know I cannot keep to myself yet I struggle with words to express. Word fail, over and over. Some are the same words I was told before yet now they paint a different picture. So how can I use the same words to say something different? Argh!

I learned so many things in the 5 years I spent in Arizona. I learned a different definition of Grace. I learned many things about people. My worldview was ginormously enlarged. Yet in that ginormousness somehow I still mattered. So many new views, thoughts, perceptions yet they were tender, young, immature.

Upon moving back to Michigan I purposed to do things differently as I protected these new things in me. That in and of itself is somewhat miraculous. The God who loves me had asked me to "leave the familiar again" so instead of returning to our previous church home we went looking for a new church home. New adventure. The place we decided upon became an enormous learning ground for me. That only brings me to another ARGH! though. I could write an entire book just on that. Again, what is important to keep? And now I'm in counseling also which has brought another entire view to things. How do I piece all these together? The work of **The Pursuer** is so elegant that putting it on paper in words feels like trying to hold running water. Once you hold it, it is no longer running. Yet I am so compelled by the elegance I've been graced with that I keep moving trying to translate invisible elegance into visible language. Reminds me of the *Darmok** episode of *"Star Trek Next Generation."* The language of the Tamarians was incomprehensible yet they wanted connection so they did not give up. A measure of success was accomplished through a sharing of a common enemy forcing them to join together. The Tamarian captain gave his life to simply begin a relationship with the Enterprise captain. They didn't completely understand yet but they did a little. Space to grow. Certain parallels to what the God who created us and pursues us has done in Jesus.

Coming along side, sharing the experience or the pain. Being truly WITH someone. These things are paramount. They change everything when they are real. When they are form or method or program without a heart truly connected I find they have the potential to foster a negative instead of the positive that is the primary aim. Without the heart engaged they are a mirage. Like my dad was to me. He was there yet I didn't know him in any remote way. My mother made certain that I knew that. I found that horribly confusing. I remember doing two things with him just him and I. My new counselor called that "sparse." I had just turned fourteen when he died. Seems like there should have been more than two. It felt like he was never there anyways – like a said, a mirage.

I felt alone my entire life until **The Pursuer** gave me my husband. He has come along side me. He chose me. We have had ups and downs, been richer or poorer, been sick and in health, times it was better and times it was worse – but we still choose to do life together. It is what binds friends together. It's what connects us to our creator who made it possible to be WITH us. That is something I get now. Him being WITH me. Looking back and seeing where he was reminds me of the movie *"The Neverending Story*."* When at the end the princess informs Atreau of all the places Bastian was with them. Atreau is panic stricken because Bastian isn't doing what Atreau thinks he should be doing but the princess understands why. The princess reminds me of **The Pursuer**. Bastian simply cannot fathom his value or the value of anything he would do. That he, one little boy had the power to change anything. That he mattered. **The Pursuer** sees our value because he gave it to us to begin with.

Which reminds me of another *"Star Trek Next Generation"* episode called *Inner Light*. A group of people inhabiting an entire planet know their star is going supernova and they cannot stop it. They value themselves and their way of life so they find a way to share who they are so they can be remembered. Because of this Captain Picard goes through an experience where he psychologically lives an entire lifetime in their culture. It accomplishes their goal and changes him forever. They even provide a souvenir – a flute that he discovers he can actually play because of his "time WITH them."

Another example of sharing is sharing pain. I noticed this profoundly in the movie *"Karate Kid"* with Jaden Smith. He's getting karate lessons from his teacher and both of them have bad attitudes until the sharing. Dre makes a surprise visit to Mr. Han who is smashing his car to smithereens and clearly distraught. Dre enters Mr. Han's pain with him and their relationship becomes completely different.

I understand that my story is just that, my story and not yours. But my hope is that you can enter my story, share in the elegance and in it see **The Pursuer** for yourself, in your story.

*The QR codes here are to elaborate for better understanding. Web addresses are provided in the Resources at the back of the book.

Short video clip of *Darmok* episode showing the inability to communicate and subsequent frustration it caused.

Short video clip from *"The Neverending Story"* where Bastian and Atreau become aware of each other and their reactions.

Short video clip of *Darmok* episode showing the sharing and subsequent understanding that follows.

Short video clip of *Innerlight* episode showing what the captain retained from the sharing.

11

bRokEn Mirrors

As I said earlier, the lies were built at home first. I didn't really know that or should I say validate that until I got my new counselor. I started counseling after beginning to write this book because I knew I would be revisiting some difficult things and thought it wise to get some assistance. It was a good decision. Previously I had turned to Christian counselors. This time I chose differently. I wanted primarily psychological help instead of spiritual. I wanted to focus on how the mind works instead of have someone tell me what I should believe. I have gotten so much more than I bargained for. I nonchalantly shared with my new counselor how I had always felt growing up and her response was unlike anything I had ever encountered before. She said *"something went terribly wrong."* And when I shared with her about bully #3 she proposed the question *"why did you believe her?"* That question had never entered my mind! Pondering it I realized that it was really the issue – that I had believed her.

How we see things, understand them, builds our beliefs. Our view. Our perception. Social Location*. Some of the things that form how we see we have control over and some things we do not. Whether or not we are seeing accurately does not alter the fact that it is the way we are seeing. We can learn and therefore change those things we can control.

One thing we cannot change is who our parents are. Whether we are raised by them or raised by someone else does not change biology. Another thing we cannot change is the past. We can learn and grow and change our perceptions but the past is etched in stone in that it did already occur. What we can change is our perspective regarding it and how we choose to move forward.

My counselor seemed shocked at the perspective that I didn't feel I belonged in my family and that I wrestled with thoughts that I had been adopted. I was stunned by her response, at her words. I had always blamed myself for such thoughts. They were just *my* stupid childish thoughts or there was something wrong with me. Surely there was no valid reason! Yet, apparently there was. Children and babies instinctively trust the love of their parents/caregivers unconditionally. They have NO fear or expectation of harm. They RUN to them – tell them everything. *"Something went terribly wrong."*

She and I discussed my upbringing in detail and things came to light that I had neatly hidden under a lie *(JAB!)*. This was very difficult to address as I considered the fall out greater than the cause to me. I had a difficult time validating it. There was no malice. How could there be harm? Everything had not been bad. Fear raged inside. If I admit and even verbalize that my need for love and security was not met as a child am I not vilifying my parents? If I allow others to know that I was terrified of my parents to the extent I'd rather sleep on the floor *(JAB!)* than wake them up when I am afraid of a simple storm what will that do? If I share the internal screams of childhood pain that were forced silent by fear *(JAB!)* in the name of the unspoken "just get over it" how will people treat me now? I need to not care. I need to use that silver bullet *"what other people think is their decision."* I cannot control how others will respond to me. I need to stop letting others control me. I need to face the truth of the failures of my parents knowing that they were just that. Personal failures due to their issues and that does not make them all bad. It does not negate the abuse and pain that was on the receiving end. No, I need to get past the wrong processing of it – where I say to myself that if it happened then it was my fault, if it happened I deserved it, if I admit it happened then I am painting a bad picture of them which is dishonoring – in essence I create a bad parent. No, the parent was the parent. What they did or didn't do was them – not me. I must see the truth – I was a child, I deserved to feel loved and protected. Their lack of affection was theirs. Their emotional distance was their emptiness. I was a child, I deserved to be curious, ask questions, discover, make mistakes. Their emotionally abusive and punitive control *(JAB!)* was their erroneous behavior passed down to them from their parents. I was a child, I had needs that deserved to be expressed and met. Their silencing of my needs was their error. I was a child, I deserved to trust, inquire, be encouraged, feel safe. The fear of my parents was not something I did wrong – it was the byproduct of something they did wrong. When I was a child my perceptions were perverted by things I did not know how to process due to being a child. I am no longer a child so I am allowing **The Pursuer** to shine his light and bring healing. I am looking in a new mirror.

My parents were not horrible people. I forgive whatever needs forgiving and choose to believe they were wounded people doing the best they knew how. Society was vastly different both in their upbringing and mine compared to now. I was born at the end of the baby boom. My father was born in 1917 which made him old enough to be my grandfather. His parents imigrated from Germany. He grew up on a potato farm and quit school after eighth grade to help with the family. His sister died when he was twenty nine years old and both his parents were dead before he married. I see that as a hard life and a lot of loss. Yet photos of him at this age show him happy. Not so much later. My mother was eleven years younger than he and born during the great depression. Her mom was born in Germany and her dad was born in Denmark. I have no idea how they met and arrived in America with her grandmother but her mom was almost deported during the war. Her dad died two months after her seventh birthday. My mother said she "was raised by her grandmother" while her mother worked. Her grandmother was born in 1875! My mother adored her grandmother. I know because she told me many times. Very rarely my mom spoke of her dad and when she did it was always negative. Maybe she was pissed at him for dying on her and the step father she ended up with but that is me guessing. She got the new step father when she was around twelve (if I remember correctly). He was a stanch Greek man and made it clear she had to pay her own way because he had his own kids from a former marriage. So she got a job as soon as she was old enough and graduated from High School as the single valedictorian. Not a lot of nurture.

My parents were very resolute, harsh and authoritarian. Things went how they said – end of story. They were the ones with the power. What we thought was irrelevant – children were to be seen and not heard. I don't think "learning styles" were discovered yet. Having learned I am a visual person has brought insight. I learn better seeing and experiencing instead of simply hearing or reading. I did not know that growing up. Not that if I knew it I think it would have mattered. I grew up hearing repeatedly *"What?! Do I need to draw you a picture?"* This of course was a rhetorical question. There was no *"yes please"* allowed. It insinuated stupidity and commanded silence *(JAB!)*. I didn't know that I **needed** that picture because I learn best through seeing and experiencing. So when I saw and experienced their anger and invalidation I learned to smile and nod whether I understood or not because questions were not allowed. I learned obedience to the authorities with the power – no questions. I learned to be powerless *(JAB!)*.

I imagine they might have thought themselves disciplinarians. I would guess it was how they were raised – although I would not know. Parents never talked about such things with their kids back then. Or if any did – mine certainly did not. Their form of "discipline" was a beating with a belt. I received beatings two times. Once for lying and the other for telling the truth. I learned to be afraid and confused *(JAB!)*. I learned to not trust what my parents said *(JAB!)*. One of my brothers was beaten so badly he could not sit for two days. He was only eight. I know there are people out there that still believe this is acceptable. I do not. I see it as abuse. I would not do that to an animal much less a human.

After my parents stopped going to church they got involved in that new hobby. Sad thing is that their hobby became our requirement. Again – they had the power and we had no choices. This new hobby was the breeding, showing and field training of Labrador Retrievers. It ruled our lives. Granted there were times we had fun with the puppies. One particular year we had two litters at the same time so one group of them we put different color yarn collars on them. I was told I could have one. I was ecstatic. I chose one. I chose the runt. He had a green collar. We called him the Jolly Green Giant. Suddenly one day without warning my dad decided to sell Jolly Green Giant even though he had been promised to me *(JAB!)*. Devastated, I was inconsolable. I hid in the big white dog house in the back yard and would not come out. My dad tried to entice me out with crunchy cheese snacks and chocolate cake snacks. That made me so angry. My view was he was trying to buy me with food *(JAB!)*. My pain was larger than those things. My dad repeated this type of cycle with one of my brothers. He was actually given one of the puppies to raise. Only to have her taken from him after one year and given to an organization to become a service animal. And not just taken from him but he was forced to do it himself. Then to "make him feel better" they took my brother out to some burger place. He was heartbroken. It didn't make him feel better. Both myself and my brother developed issues regarding food. Perhaps a love/hate thing because food did not fix our heart issues.

Over the years it became very apparent to me that I had "daddy issues." These issues have been a huge obstacle in seeing God as a loving Father. Multiple times I have addressed them as best I knew how and each time I thought I was free until it was apparent I was not. My counselor asked me how I saw my dad. Without hesitation I said a mirage. He was there but not there. He loved the dogs. I did not remember any demonstrations of affection or any "I love you's" *(JAB!)*. I don't remember "daddy." I only remember those two times I had ever done anything with my dad – just him and me – I went to a hardware store with him when I was five and he bought me a caroler tree topper (that I still have), and later a girl's organization bowling event where we left before it was over and we won a trophy for last place. As I said my counselor used the word "sparse" for time with my dad. No one had ever validated that before. That is when I saw photos of him in my mind and felt that painful yearning.

Even though my house is neat and uncluttered I have discovered I have trouble separating from photos and mementos *(JAB!)*. I asked my counselor about emotional/memory hoarding. It is not an official thing but she notated that it may be an area that needs to be studied. It came out that perhaps my things I have kept are attached to trying get what I can never have – a relationship with my dad. She said I had a hole and had grown around it. But it can never be removed. What was not, cannot become – my dad is gone. The love was wanting and cannot be obtained. The photo cannot give me what I desire so much. There is only loss. Loss not only of my actual dad, but I must grieve and let go of the dad I wish I had but never did. There is only going forward. She notated the relationship I have with my husband being 180 from my dad and how "intuitive" I was to choose the man I did. I told her it wasn't me but it was **The Pursuer** protecting me and blessing me. She said it is fortunate I didn't repeat the pain by marrying an emotionally unavailable man like many people do. I am indeed fortunate.

After this enlightening counseling session a deep grief got triggered by something I saw on TV *(JAB!)*. A little girl and her daddy. I had a meltdown. I told my counselor I don't want this to keep happening. She compared it to an ankle injury she had sustained and how it is healed now and doesn't stop her yet sometimes when the weather is bad she feels something and remembers. My upbringing is a part of me and I will remember but I need to not return to the core of the wound and then we talked about grieving. I thought of the part of that process – anger – I said

I think I needed permission to be angry. That was enlightening to me. I had taught grief recovery. What was going on? Why could I not do what I taught? I was that child looking for someone outside of me to tell me it was ok to be angry. I didn't believe it was ok to feel angry – that would be "bad," I would get "in trouble" *(JAB!)*. Feelings. That's another issue.

I talked about my difficulty in identifying what was true, really happened, am I making it up? *(JAB!)* I discovered evidence of another thing I did with my dad alone but I don't remember going, what is true?? *(JAB!)* Was I making a big deal out of nothing? *(JAB!)* Was I perverting reality? *(JAB!)* What was right? *(JAB!)* She told me to stop trying so hard to be right. She sorted it into parts. She said we can be pretty certain that my dad was no hero but could he have loved me? He may have but that is not the issue exactly. The issue is my perception is very real. Perception is reality. He may have just been operating out of his background of German immigrant, farmer and been stoic with the put up or shut up kind of survival attitude, common for immigrants especially back then. So the reality of did he or didn't he is not really the issue. We discussed my difficulty validating this as I continually compare to what I consider valid traumas like 9/11 etc. She said yes this is not 9/11 but the issue is my perception and the reality that what I needed was not provided. We don't negate my need because it wasn't taken care of. No malice ≠ No harm. I was a child and I didn't know, understand and could not process what was happening so I reframed it in what seemed logical. This is what kids do. I carried this into adulthood and now it is coming to light. I need to grieve the dad I didn't have, the fake one I created in my mind with a child's coping mechanism. The fake dad. That really hit home. Because I couldn't validate my loss I created a fake dad in my head. This has continuously effected my perception of God. Blinded me to **The Pursuer.** I felt fatherless before my dad died. I saw him as a mirage before he died and kept a mirage after. I used that same word regarding the promises of God with my first counselor many years ago. This fed the bull's-eye way back at that church.

I talked with her about a video I had watched about bullying. It was a very good video validating how damaging bullying is and standing up to it etc. However she pointed out to me what I took away from that was the "get over it" part. Putting that on myself. She talked about a scar in me that is still not healed that seems to be the prevailing issue – identifying feelings and invalidated feelings. She believes that this goes back to my preverbal years when a child learns what their feeling are and what to do with them. How a parent mirrors to the child what they are feeling, validates it and then helps the child address it. This is where she inserts the *"something went terribly wrong."* These seem to be things I clearly have difficulty with. Apparently my parental mirror was broken also. She notated that when I arrived I was not able to put into words what I was feeling – epic fail for words. She was somewhat surprised at that because she says I am an articulate woman. Yet this topic has been throughout all my sessions – that I don't know what I am feeling or what to do with it.

So WHAT went terribly wrong?? This time frame is before I would have a memory. I went looking for photographs that showed my mom or dad holding me, smiling at me, something. To my great sadness I found none. However I did discover that my dad's maternal grandfather died when my mom was six months pregnant with me. Plus she was dealing with an unplanned pregnancy. Maybe she got depressed?? I found information that said if mothers are depressed after having their babies they could possibly become emotionally unavailable to the newborn. If this happens they can be unable to connect and this can have a negative impact on the baby's development. Someone who is "emotionally unavailable" is unable to share their feelings and validate your feelings. If this is prolonged it actually effects the chemical make-up of the child's brain. The emotional exchanges that moms and babies share actually increase the brain growth and function through something called affective sharing.

In research I found the effects of an emotionally unavailable mother on children is that they may feel guilty for feeling happy, take on excess responsibility. They may see ordinary emotions as extreme or dangerous. They may have deep-seated beliefs where they see other people's needs as more important than their own and feel they cannot trust anyone to "be there" for them. They may frequently discount the importance of their own feelings and feel guilty when others are unhappy as if it was their fault. I have dealt with all of those.

While researching the above I also found information regarding a controlling mother. Had I not stumbled upon that information I would not have gone looking. That term sounds bad to the "good child" I was raised to be. However I found those side effects in me also. Choice was not something I believed I held as something that belonged to me. What I thought, felt, wanted or needed seemed irrelevant or inappropriate. It was always subject to any of the authorities with the power, not just my mother. Crying was considered manipulative so unless I had what "they" considered to be a valid reason it was not allowed. Needs were defined as roof over your head, food on the table, clothes to wear. Wants were selfish. I did not know the difference between who I was required to be and who I really was.

Who I was, I did not see. All the mirrors were broken.

I had read a book on trauma back during that particular year/ year and half of healing that the God who loved me walked me through. Reading it helped a lot at that time but I still wrestled with discounting it in my heart. When I was looking for a counselor I discovered there were ones trained regarding trauma. Hmm. That led me to the discovery that childhood trauma* is much different than adult trauma. Hmm. I did some study on childhood trauma and found much validation I needed. I had not considered how young I was when any of the things happened to me growing up. I had not understood age was a factor in and of itself giving the potential for severe and long lasting effects. The string of traumas happened at multiple and various ages and stages of my development. The fact that a string occurred is identified as a trauma in and of itself *(JAB!)*. Instead of a traumatic experience preparing a child for a subsequent one it is more apt to cause intensified reactions each time. Trauma overwhelms a person's ability to cope, disrupts the equilibrium in the body and causes excess action in the nervous system *(JAB!)*. Repeated trauma causes repetitive overwhelming to both the conscious and subconscious mind *(JAB!)*. Responses are called hyperarousal and dissociation. Reading what those are I see myself very clearly as having gone through dissociation. Unresolved childhood trauma carries a fundamental sense of fear and helplessness into adulthood *(JAB!)*. I am in process of healing and making good progress. I am thankful to learn some reason for lapses in memory surrounding the traumas. I don't remember ninth grade at all after my dad died. **The Pursuer** graciously unveiled the majority of this chapter after I had begun counseling. I was gently ushered through. I was not alone. I have been validated instead of re-traumatized. Had I become aware of some of this prior I believe it may have been detrimental. **The Pursuer** is gentle.

No, the teacher's shaming and humiliating of me when I was barely six is not the same as the Sandy Hook massacre. No, the subsequent string of various emotional woundings and traumas is not the same as a tsunami. No, the malfunction of love and the invalidation of my personhood by my parents is not the same as a plane crash. No, the spiritual orphaning by the religious leaders is not the same as the holocaust. You cannot compare them. Trauma is personal. It does not disappear if it is not validated. When it is ignored or invalidated the silent screams continue internally heard only by the one held captive. When someone enters the pain and hears the screams healing can begin.

*The QR codes here are to elaborate for better understanding. Web addresses are provided in the Resources at the back of the book.

If you are unfamiliar with the term social location, this is the best article/paper I have found to explain it by Dr. David Rhoads.

"Effect Of Traumatic Events On Children" by Bruce D Perry, MD, Ph.D.

12

Puzzle Pieces

కావాలికి

When you look at ALL the pieces of a puzzle in a box it looks like a disorganized mess. But knowing it is a puzzle you know each piece has a place it belongs. Each piece is important yet no piece can stand alone. Some pieces "appear" more intriguing or important even before they are placed in the big picture. With one of these you might try and try to find where it goes but cannot so you throw it back in the box frustrated. Sometimes with a large puzzle it appears one section goes with another until you get a certain connecting piece. With this new piece you exclaim "aha!" and see how it fits perfectly in another spot. This is a way I am seeing many parts of my life. Here are some key puzzle pieces that I became aware of at various points in time. **The Pursuer** pieced things together. Some have already been placed in the puzzle and perhaps mentioned already. Some are recently found and/or still in the box.

Titus 3:5 & 6 KJV – This one was pointed out by the God who saved me way back when I lived in that little flat above Mrs. Brady. I instantly memorized it but I didn't really understand it at the time. It was one of those "intriguing" pieces of the puzzle that I "threw back in the box." It says *"not by works of righteousness which we have done, but according to his mercy he saved us, by the washing of regeneration, and renewing of the Holy Ghost, which he shed on us abundantly..."* I get it now. Now I know that I am the righteousness of God because I have received **The Pursuer's** gift of righteousness because of His abundant grace.

Story of Legion – For a long time I wanted to be a missionary and I was told no using a story in the Bible. It was the story of the guy that Jesus freed from a bunch of demons. What Jesus told that guy was what I believed the God who saved me told me. To go back to your friends and family and publish all God has done. I tried. Numerous times I aimed for going into full time ministry and um, somehow, didn't. Now it is clear to me that **The Pursuer** was involved in that. Now I am writing this book – hmm.

Mistakes – At that ladies retreat I told you about **The Pursuer** spoke to my heart regarding mistakes. He said *"I'm going to teach you how to make mistakes."* I internally freaked out. Fear and panic, surprise, shock and other emotions washed over me. I felt like he said he was going to teach me how to sin. But that is not what he said. I was intensely fearful of mistakes which always presented themselves as failure – every time. It would sometimes send me into quite the tizzy. People would say to me *"Don't be so hard on yourself"* but all I heard was more condemnation *(JAB!)*. I had no idea how to process that statement. I prayed. Little by little **The Pursuer** provided multiple pieces. One piece wasn't enough. Grace upon grace, mercy overflowing. I learned making a mistake is not sinful, is not the end of the world. Even a failure is not the end of the world or sinful. There is no execution set. Breathe. Relax. What IS useful is for me to see, to get up, and to keep going. Learn. That thing called *"The Serenity Prayer"* fits very nicely here.

Safe group – A small group of us gathered at my friend Renee's apartment to watch the video series of the book *"Boundaries."* It was a place we all committed to as being safe to share. Safe meaning we told no one outside the group any details of what we discussed. Privacy. In this gathering is where I first shared my feelings of intense lack of value – that I did not feel I had the right to even exist. I was not only encouraged but one other member of the group opened up that they felt that way also. I was not alone. Here I learned that safety and trust in relationship beyond my husband is actually possible. I would call this piece an edge piece or maybe even a corner piece.

Be a solution person – I got this piece from a sermon I heard when we were out of town. We visited a relative's church. A solution person does not ignore the problem, does not deny there is a problem. A problem MUST be recognized, validated. Being a solution person is one who sees and validates that there is a problem but does not park there. The next step is to look for, find and implement a solution! This is full of hope. I knew exactly where this piece went.

My daughter's question – Apparently I was very verbally negative regarding my growing up to my daughter. One day she retorted a question to me that rattled me to action and rightly so. She said to me, *"Didn't anything good ever happen to you?"* Wow – interesting question I asked myself again and again. I was trapped in the negative. I went looking for good and found some. She helped me have a better attitude in addressing the truth. A very important piece indeed.

"I don't know how!" – Sometime while living in Arizona I had an epiphany that turned into a breakthrough. We encountered many challenges out there and I was apparently worrying and unaware of it. When talking with the pastor's wife before church one day she told me to *"cast my care."* Out of my mouth came words that shocked me. Feeling utterly powerless I lamented *"I don't know how!"* Those words echoed inside of me bringing the light I needed. I poured out my heart to the God who loves me asking him to teach me. **The Pursuer** answered with lavish help. This was a section of the puzzle.

The S.O.S. rock – Before moving to Arizona I was a part of a group of ladies called S.O.S. that gathered monthly in various people's homes. We came from all different backgrounds and denominations to support each other and share Jesus. My friend Stephanie that headed it up is very creative and often did object lessons. One particular evening she had a bag of small rocks and she talked about God being our rock. We were instructed to choose a rock out of the bag to be a reminder to us. As I was choosing mine **The Pursuer** spoke to my heart in that "clear as day" sort of way. The words gently were *"you're gonna really need that."* Of course due to where I was in my process at the time those words scared me even though I knew they were meant to help me. I chose my small rock more intentionally. I carried that rock with me for the next few years as we proceeded to move and go through many difficult circumstances and emotions. It spoke comfort to me when my heart was overwhelmed with fear. It reminded me I was not alone. This is a corner piece.

Revelation knowledge – I had heard this term many times and had some understanding of it and even had received some of it. But then I guess you'd say I got a revelation about revelation. Ha ha – sounds ridiculous I know. Anyways, what it is, is something **The Pursuer** unveils, reveals, something you just KNOW, you SEE it, it's plain as day so to speak. When that happens – no one can tell you different and *the JAB!* cannot take it away. That kind of knowing gives me strength and is easy to share because I don't have to try to remember it – I just know. I want and need more of this. Many pieces of the puzzle that belong in varying places – some I haven't found yet.

"Just walk across the room" – People think various things when they hear the word evangelism. Probably the first thing I would think of was "pressure." That clearly was not working for me. I had done many of the common things like cold calls, going door to door, participated in plays and other productions etc. In them I carried this internal crushing pressure that if I didn't lead someone to Jesus they would go to hell and it would be all my fault *(JAB!)* and then the voice of the bull's-eye *(JAB!)* silently followed because I didn't know it was there. I got free of this pressure through a message my pastor in Arizona delivered. He called it *"just walk across the room"* and it was so simple, so relaxed. Previously I felt what I knew was inadequate as I felt I had to have every answer to any question anyone would have and be able to answer any argument. I'm pretty sure that is not what I was taught but the wounds in me perverted the truth *(JAB!)*. Previously I didn't understand process either. Here he was saying to simply begin a conversation (about anything) with a person and if your conversation leads to another conversation that's awesome. He was saying to trust the Holy Spirit

regarding whatever was said and when. Again, I'm pretty sure I was probably taught that at the church I went to before we moved to Arizona but again, the wounds perverted the truth *(JAB!)* and those five little words somehow untwisted it making it just having a nice relaxed conversation led by **The Pursuer.** He knows if we should talk about him or about the weather. This is the piece you find after you walk away and come back with fresh eyes.

"I love people. They want me to talk to them" – Reading that you may think that sounds ridiculous. It was life changing to me. While working in Arizona, **The Pursuer** opened my eyes to something I had not realized before. I would see people at work congregating and talking and I would feel left out and afraid. **The Pursuer** showed me one reason why – I had a fear of intimacy with people that kept me from talking to them, especially if it was a group. Somehow one on one wasn't too difficult but the more people the larger the fear. **The Pursuer** gave me those ten words to rehearse every morning to change my perspective and build courage in me. Later he also added *"God loves people. He wants me to talk to them."* More connecting pieces.

A dream – I've had many dreams that I have recorded. Some have just been silly. Some have had lessons in them for me. One was of my mother after she passed that brought me comfort. But about three years ago, while in Arizona I had a very intriguing dream. I wrote it down with as much detail as I could and then prayed about it because it was odd and it just "felt" like it was important. I knew two people in it but their names and their roles were what was important. I ended up with sort of a moral of the story or a tag line. It was *"Grace brings you in and Glory establishes."* I had absolutely no idea what that meant at the time so that piece got thrown back in the box. Last year a ministry we are partners with had a focus called "great grace." We learned so very much about grace which brought us into many new things. This year we have been directed to a focus of "greater glory" through a different ministry. Hmm I pulled that piece back out of the box to see where it goes. I have a better idea but not completely certain.

Courage – As I said in The ARGGHHH when I returned to Michigan I sought to protect the new things I had learned in Arizona. That required me to speak up where I had previously been silent or compliant. It was scary but each time I did this was a victory. People close to me began to notice these little victories. Still working on larger victories. I had been looking for this piece for a very long time.

Effortless – After returning to MI our new pastor used this word to describe how we are to follow Jesus. Seriously? My concept was the opposite and I wanted this new one. I started hearing this concept more from other sources also. They said that REAL change is effortless. Change that you work for is change you must maintain. I knew that very well by experience. I wanted this effortless experience. I pursued this. I learned about a thing called "rest." I discovered a new mirror! Another major piece to the puzzle.

Not because of me – At this new church I heard the pastor say some thing I had never heard before that rocked my world beyond words. He said that we need a savior not because of our sin but because of Adam's sin. Adam sinned and that was passed down to all of us. I had heard that in different words before but somehow those particular words separated that word "sin" from me and my fault and my behavior and my, my… That changed it to sin was an issue that needed to be dealt with separately from me. That made sin not a behavior but rather a place, or position, or state of being. Jesus came and took that thing called sin, paid off what it had cost, in full, for all time, providing total forgiveness by his blood – making us "guilty" of right standing with God. Something He did that I could not Undo. It was more like take it or leave it. A piece I had not been able to locate but a friend found it for me.

As much as Jesus? – I wrote earlier how I heard a minister say that God loves us as much as he loves Jesus and how I didn't understand. I threw that piece back. However this became an issue over a few months during our move back to Michigan as I heard it repeated over and over and each time it brought pain. Like continuously picking up the same puzzle piece trying to put it in the wrong place. I didn't understand. I did not know that it was somehow linked to that bull's-eye and to that lie about the sparrow. When I heard them say that God loved me as much as he loved Jesus my insides recoiled "but he killed Jesus" or "he sent him to die"… It connected to death not life in my soul. It brought fear not joy. By the grace of **The Pursuer** I used the puzzle piece of courage and asked the pastor about this. He directed me to learn how much the Father loved Jesus, about their relationship. Thankfully I listened. I came to learn the LOVE I had never seen. It was something unveiled – revealed. The Father did not kill Jesus. He protected him from every attack. He lacked nothing. Nobody "murdered" Jesus – that was not possible. He is God who came in the flesh. The Father in love for us gave Jesus a human body – let him enter our pain. Jesus proceeded to demonstrate that love for us by giving us his life – allowing us the ability to enter His pain – the loss of us. We have been given the opportunity to choose to share this relationship of love. This LOVE – It's freaking amazing! What a beautiful piece indeed.

Convinced – I have a thing I call quiet time every day where I pray and stuff. One day while having this time **The Pursuer** opened my eyes to show me that I had become convinced – finally. Being convinced of the Love of God for ME. That nothing could separate me from his love – nothing. **Unconditional LOVE.** No fine print. No restrictions. No "you better not screw up." No demands. No requirements. My heart soared like Rudolph the red nosed reindeer flew after Clarice said she thought he was cute. But like the other characters in that cartoon weren't so happy with Rudolph my heart raged against me railing "what took you so long?...." One of those pieces that is really cool but has something on it you can't make out.

Identity – I kept picking up this one piece thinking it fit but it didn't. Growing up I looked into numerous broken mirrors to identify who I was. Some passive, some aggressive but none free. **The Pursuer** apprehended me for freedom. I didn't understand so in my previous mode of operation I looked to the authorities I perceived had the power for them to tell me who I was. I heard I had to die to self and be dead in Christ but then I was gonna live but then not I but it was Christ who would live. What the heck does that mean? I did not understand where "I" went if indeed "I" was allowed to exist. But if I was not allowed to exist then why did he bother to do anything? Many times I would be told that my identity was Christ. Either they didn't understand what I was asking or I didn't understand what they were telling me. It was erasing me and somehow that seemed wrong. I had tried to do that myself and knew it was wrong. A way **The Pursuer** helped me to understand was using the word "hidden." Have you ever hidden something to protect it because it was such an important thing? Have you ever seen a person hide a child behind them to protect them from danger of some sort? Those are the pictures he gave me. I am me, created by him with unique traits and quirks that I get to discover and identify. When I ask him about them he teaches me how they work, what they are for. No one else is like me. Likewise, no one else is like you. We are like snowflakes. Unique by design and glistening by his glory. This is my favorite piece, for I am WE – perfect in him and never alone.

Tone of voice – This beautiful piece is actually composed of two that were elegantly combined. I didn't know they were even a part of the puzzle until someone found them for me. I think they fell on the floor. The first one was handed to me by a friend Phil. It was regarding misinterpreting what God is trying to tell us because we filter it through what we believe about ourselves or our lack of trust of Him. We hear inaccurately. That very night I experienced it on a tiny level but big enough for me to see. **The Pursuer's** tone is one of love and encouragement, convincing us we are good enough, we are righteous because of Jesus. He is called the Comfort-er, the Help-er. Not the faultfinder. The second piece was handed to me by my counselor when I was lamenting why, why, why has it taken me so long to believe the UNconditional love of God? She said that she believed God was not impatient with me but that I was. That perhaps it needed to take that long. Perhaps I could change my tone from judgment to curiosity. Wow – that was enlightening. Same words, different tone – grace.

Paint by numbers – This piece was also found by my counselor and part of the section where the tone of voice pieces go. Wrestling with how long and what's important and not wanting to negate good but needing to validate harm – argh! It was the same day I had that conversation at lunch with my friend who echoed my difficulty with those years. My new counselor proposed that perhaps I had learned much but it was put together like a paint by numbers rather than an elegant masterpiece. Something in me knew that was accurate yet it took me a while to process because that still sounded negative to that "good child." But think about it. When you are young those paint by number things are so cool. Then you learn there is a more excellent way. That's the way of **The Pursuer.**

My son's question – When we lived in Arizona and we were addressing some difficult things my son asked me a question that I knew the answer was "no" but also knew there was something more there. It was one of those questions a person could get angry at if it was heard as accusing instead of inquiring. His tone was drenched in the love of **The Pursuer.** He asked me if my children were an idol to me. As I said, I answered no – correctly… but. So I made it a matter of prayer. It took much longer than I'd like to admit but it was a process to get to what was appearing as that yet was not that. One morning in that thing I call quiet time **The Pursuer** revealed it to me. I did not esteem my children higher than Him. No, what I had done was erroneously find my identity in them. Yes they were gifts from **The Pursuer** and being a mom is a role. It was like I became the role. As much as I had attempted to prepare to not be "one of them" – those moms that have a nervous breakdown when empty nest occurs, I still had a negative side effect. One I had not been aware of so did not address. I understood being told that, but still knew there was more to the story. The "good mom" (I'll call her) was a "good child" looking for a grown up. I need to be that grown up. I'm in process of growing up that "good child" to stand on her own two feet so to speak. This piece goes with many of the ones listed above – primarily identity.

Microsurgery – I was pondering all the deep work in my soul that was being done, all the counseling etc. and this word came to me. I had to go and see if it was an actual word or actual medical thing – it is and it is amazing. **The Pursuer** has been doing this in my heart. But I also learned that before microsurgery is performed there is a necessary preparation. This really spoke to me about my long process. One of the stories I read talked about a severe injury involving broken bones with open flesh that was contaminated by dirt, grass and whatnot. They had to remove the foreign materials, spray wash it with gallons of antibiotic fluid and then needed to pack it with some kind of beads saturated with antibiotics just to fight infection. They repeated this surgical treatment until the wound was infection free. Only then did they begin the permanent reconstruction. Then followed the healing and rehabilitation. It was a long involved and painful process. I could visualize the analogy of this process in me. All that removing and cleaning and packing, repeat – I saw all those years of learning and growing before we moved to Arizona. I thought of the times I had felt overwhelmed by information. It was more than I could process – too much too fast. I felt like a canary getting a drink from a fire hose. The flushing of the wound in the microsurgery prep made sense of that. It helped address the negative feelings of why this has taken so long. It wasn't that I had failed to learn, it was preparation for the deeper, more precise work of **The Pursuer.** This whole process is another major portion of the puzzle.

Full Recovery – **The Pursuer** has spoken to me on this subject in various ways multiple times over the years. First time I recall is when I got my wedding ring replaced and He spoke of restoring *"the years the locust had eaten."* I think I was superficial in my understanding at that time. Again I perceived it after beginning to sing at our church out in Arizona. A friend even gave me a paper with a "confession" (something for me to read out loud daily) that speaks of restoration and favor. I seemed to be more attentive to the favor part. Then the year we returned from Arizona I was instructed by the God who loves me to say a specific confession. I laughed the first time I read it. It was the opposite of what was going on in my life at the time. It began with *"This is going to be the finest most outstanding year we have ever experienced.."* I had just gone through three devastating things. Are you freaking kidding me???? But graciously and gently **The Pursuer** addressed my recoiling, I obeyed and the results are beyond amazing. It changed my thinking process. It changed my expectation. *"Restoration of all that was lost"* was part of it. That was saying all *the JAB!* stole will be restored. This is a section of the puzzle. I have found numerous pieces already but there are more to find.

No Malice ≠ No Harm – This is a difficult puzzle piece to find. Some of the things that happened to me I see malice. Like my first grade teacher, bully #3, that mob that met me at school and the spirit behind those religious leaders. But the others I do not see or ascribe malice or an intention to harm – like my parents, other family members, teachers or pastors. They are people. People make mistakes. So I would tend to negate and invalidate the negative effect because I could not wrap my head around if it wasn't intentional then it couldn't harm. Maybe hurt, but not harm. Even considering the hurt I had difficulty with as I tended to place all blame on myself like a child. But talking with my counselor she told me it is not all black or all white – there is grey. People are not all bad or all good and people can change. Like my mom and

I became friends. Then I watched an episode of *"Hoarders Buried Alive."* The woman had two sons and was in danger of them being taken away by Child Protective Services. They were preteen/early teens. Her house was disgustingly unsanitary/unhealthy and dangerous (electrical – high danger of fire). Her lack of self-value and untrue beliefs were ginormous and very obvious. She did not see that she was harming her sons. It was clear that she believed she loved them. They believed she loved them also and loved her, yet they were showing signs of harm. She had no malice yet harm was quite evident. Help is what changed the story. Someone entered her pain and she got better and was able to keep her kids who also got help.

Sharing – Loneliness* is a horrible feeling. A person does not need to be alone to feel lonely. It is a matter of the heart. I have felt lonely in a room full of people. A person can feel it when they are unable to connect or communicate adequately, or worse, forbidden to communicate things of importance. I believe we are designed for connection. Heart to heart connection is euphoric. But it takes courage to invite someone into our heart – to share. Being rejected is distressing. Feeling disconnected is agonizing. It strikes at our personhood. Seeks to reduce our value in our perception. I learned a term in counseling that has helped me – "alone-ness." My counselor said we all have a certain "alone" ness where it is just us by our self that is only ours. The "I" in identity if you will. I find it difficult to explain but I understood what she was saying. In this aloneness we have the ability to invite **The Pursuer.** This inviting piece goes with the piece called courage.

Compassion Was Born

God came   to see   behind   our eyes
To feel   **our** feelings
To see   **our** sights
To correct the wrongs
And provide the rights
He came to see   behind our eyes

God became **human**
I don't understand
How **can** it be
God with **us**
God **in** us
God **for** us
Can we   believe
Can we   embrace
Can we **allow** him his rightful place
He came to see   behind our eyes

The one   who **made** us
The one   who **reigns**
He **understands** us
All of our pains
All of our fears
All of our thoughts
Can we **believe**
Can we **embrace**

Can we allow him his **rightful place**
He came to see behind our eyes

The love that he **showed**
The love he **displays**
Will we **receive** it
Will we **give** it away

We **marvel**
We **ponder**
We fear and we fret
What does this mean
What do we do
He came   to see   behind   our eyes

He gave – give
He loved – love
He endured – don't give up
He knew **us** – know him

He **came** to see behind our eyes
Come - and see behind his
Go - and see behind others

Miracle   after   miracle
He did
Just to come
Did you **see**
Did you **notice**
Look!

*The QR codes here are to elaborate for better understanding. Web addresses are provided in the Resources at the back of the book.

 "Loneliness Is More Dangerous Than We Thought" article by Beth Greenfield

 It takes courage to share. This untitled poem by Aaron Sorkin illustrates well that true help comes from truly sharing.

13

New Mirror

๛◉๖

Trading old broken mirrors that feed lies into our souls for new mirrors of freedom requires choices. Daily, repetitive choices. Some come easier than others but every new choice is a victory. Every victory whether large or small deserves to be celebrated. Others may not see our victories the same way we do. We know what we used to do. They only see what is now. Unless we have shared. Unless they have entered our pain and found compassionate understanding. Then they celebrate with us.

I have finally learned that I matter. I am not simply tolerated by that God guy, as I knew him long ago. I am celebrated. Yes celebrated. I was celebrated back then, but I did not know it. That bull's-eye is a lie. I deserve His love because He said so. There is no earning, only receiving. I matter just because I'm breathing. I have a new mirror for the story Jesus shared about the ninety nine sheep and going after the one. HE went after the sheep. HE found the sheep. HE placed the sheep on his shoulders and carried it. HE brought the sheep home rejoicing and inviting others to join. HE then talks about repentance. What the heck did the sheep do? I see no groveling. I see no change of behavior. I see no promising to be good. I see the sheep LET the shepherd find him. I see the sheep LET the shepherd carry him. I see the sheep LET the shepherd love him. Valued and loved. You matter just as much as I do. Coming to know that, being convinced of it, changes everything.

I have learned that I have a right to feel what I feel even if someone else does not like it or I cannot find the words to describe or explain. That is still not easy for me yet but I'm practicing. I have learned that I have a right to have needs, communicate them and to be heard. Having needs is not evidence of weakness – it is human. Needs met feed our wellbeing. They are individual and relative. Everyone deserves to have their needs met. I am learning to identify them in my life. I believe that the unmet needs in our lives talk. They talk trash *(JAB!)*. **The Pursuer** has it recorded that our creator is our source and abundant supply. If you're anything like I was you might scoff at that saying that is a really nice story I wish that it was true in my life. I had been taught much about that and I understood English for a long time. I even believed it to a point but that bull's-eye was in the way – it's gone now. I had to learn how much I was loved before I could really grab ahold of being well cared for. I have learned about something called The Blessing. It has revolutionized our lives.

I am learning to "step away" from myself as my counselor calls it to observe and learn myself. To identify what I want and what I think instead of what I have previously conformed to out of fear. I need to take time to listen to myself and notice what appeals to me, attracts me, feels easy or comfortable – learn.

New Mirror

I came across the following poem while still in Arizona and began rehearsing it. Since I began doing this I have progressively altered my copy as I grow and need to change it to adapt to the place I am in my journey. Here is the original.

You can't be all things to all people
You can't do all things at once
You can't do all things equally well
You can't do all things better than everyone else
Your humanity is showing just like everyone else's

So you have to find out who you are, and be that
You have to decide what comes first, and do that
You have to discover your strengths, and use them
You have to learn not to compete with others
Because no one else is in the contest of *being you*

Then you will have learned to accept your own uniqueness
You will have learned to set priorities and make decisions
You will have learned to live with your limitations
You will have learned to give yourself the respect that is due
And you'll be a most vital human

Dare to believe that you are a wonderful, unique person
That you are a once-in-all-history event
That it's more than a right, it's your duty, to be who you are
That life is not a problem to solve, but a gift to cherish
And you'll be able to stay one up on what used to get you down.
-author unknown

I still have more to learn on how to make different choices as I apply all I have learned and am learning. I have collected some of

175

my victories. Some are small and some are large. Some might seem silly to you but may actually be huge to me. I am taking my puzzle piece of courage and my puzzle piece of sharing and laying them together here. They are different choices I have made or different responses I have noticed. I am hoping you celebrate with me and are inspired in your life.

Laughed at myself:

Laughing at myself was something I did not know how to do. I had been told to do it but was crippled to pull it off. I saw other people do that and wished I could. Well one day I took my mother in law to one of her doctors for an appointment like I usually do. This particular time I took her to the wrong building - DUH! Head slap / laugh. I laughed out loud. I thought it was hilarious. I even told other people what a daft thing I did and how funny it was. What an awesome victory. What a wonderful freedom to have.

Courage, Observe, Learn:

While we were out of town my husband and I visited a church. We usually did not do that. We don't know anyone and the thought itself would be uncomfortable. But this time I wanted to visit for the reason of seeing from a different view and broadening my perspective on what is called "the body of Christ." That in itself is a growth/victory – putting myself in a situation for emotional challenge simply for the challenge itself. My expectations were clearly inaccurate. The culture of the church was older, the size was much much smaller, assistance negligible, warmth was void, geared for spectator which made worship dull even though the music was high quality/ performance (felt like a concert). Had we not stopped to ask directions we would have engaged no one who "worked" there. Two people said hi, one when we were told to say hi. How did I fare? I recognized it to be a valid church to meet the needs of people who are not like me and made the decision to gather whatever good I could in spite of the atmosphere I didn't care for. No judgment, no fear, no condemnation. People are different and need different things. This is a victory on so many levels. The courage to go in the first place. The courage to stay when uncomfortable. The respect for them to be who they are even if it wasn't "my flavor." The respect for me to not have to like it. Happy dance time.

New response:

My husband and I went to an indoor range to shoot hand guns. I had not done this in a few years and had a gun I had never used before at a range I'd never been to. I asked at the rental counter if I would receive help/instruction before shooting and was told yes. When I got inside the range the man spoke fast and without any concern for our understanding of what he said. Just rattling it off like a robot to move on to the next. We made him repeat himself which he did not like. Then I asked for help to load my gun. He was irritated to be asked and with a quite condescending attitude rushed through the process with no regard for my understanding or retaining what he had just said. He then displayed such a "move along lady" attitude. It frustrated me. I didn't remember all he said so I didn't know how to proceed completely. I got parts but was definitely not comfortable. I "moved along" into the range area. The staple gun to attach my target was jammed. I was able to find another and then figure out how to attach my target to the mount. I struggled but finally loaded the bullets in the magazine but they were in there backwards. My husband helped me remedy the situation and I proceeded to shoot and load and shoot, etc. I tried my husband's gun but it hurt to shoot so I went back to mine. After we were done I said to my husband *"I had fun. Everyone is a beginner sometime. "* Right after I said that, I had the revelation of how profound it was for me to say that. I did not have any shred of condemnation for the lack of understanding I had or the mistakes I made. I celebrated. As I write this now I still see old thinking there. Perhaps today I might say to the rude man – *"Hey! Don't you brush me off. I asked if I would get help and was told yes. You need to help me. It is your job. "* Or perhaps I would talk to the manager regarding his employee's lack of customer service. Still the initial response was a victory from former thinking.

Fear and Belonging:

I made the decision to go to a ladies breakfast by myself when I really wanted to have someone come with me. I chose to put myself in that uncomfortable situation and take responsibility for how I felt and decisions I was going to make. Upon arriving (too early) I went in and looked around – found no seat. The people I "know" and would "like" to sit with are working the event and not sitting. I took my coat to the car giving myself more time and refused the negative feelings that were trying to get me to leave *(JAB!)*. This put me in the right place to have an encouraging conversation with someone in the parking lot. Grace. Entering again I still found no seat but got a cup of coffee and refused negative thoughts feeding negative feelings and fear *(JAB!)*. This put me in the situation where I was introduced to someone I did not know and had a nice chat. I went to look again for a place I'd be comfortable to sit but still no seat and still in control in my mind and therefore of my feelings also. I just stood there until they started talking about the procedure for getting our food. I continued to refuse fearful thoughts and prayed. Soon someone I knew came in and we greeted. I asked if they had a seat and if I could sit with them. She pointed to a table saying there were four seats. I was not aware she had her daughters with her. My original plan was to sit next to her, someone I knew, at a table of people I don't know. Thinking of me. But instead of acting out the self-centered plan I sat three seats from her so her daughters could sit next to her and then me next to the "stranger" who became a friend by the end of breakfast. After sitting there I discovered someone else I knew at the table even though I had not seen them earlier. She and I sat together for the second part of the event. This was especially difficult because it took so much repetitive inner intent. But I won and I danced in my heart.

I didn't freak out x 3:

One day while I was working on this book my computer suddenly had an issue and just went into restart. I had just cut a portion to paste on another file and had not pasted it. It was seemingly lost in this technology glitch *(JAB!)*. I didn't freak out. I considered I "might" have the original information but was not certain. I noted vaguely what I remembered of what I had cut and then just moved on. I discovered there was a "recovered" file as well as the original at the last time I saved it. In the original the portion I had cut to paste was still there. I didn't lose anything – not the info – not my peace. Glory to God.

The same day I went to drop off some donations. I got a receipt. When I got home I couldn't find the receipt. I looked in the car and it wasn't there. I considered I may have dropped it in the store where I had stopped *(JAB!)*. However I didn't freak out. I looked again finding other receipts I had not put where they belonged. I looked again where I thought I had put it and found it at the bottom of the pocket. I didn't lose anything – not the receipt – not my peace. Glory to God.

I had been praying about a possible ministry or outreach for quite a while. I was having much difficulty deciphering this "thing" I had inside me. On this particular day I was planning on starting a blog in an effort to just keep moving. I had never done a blog and really had no clue. After having decided on where to host the blog and what theme to start with, which in itself was a large task for me, I clicked to begin. However when I entered the name I wanted I was denied. It was reserved *(JAB!)*. Discouragement wanted in but I didn't freak out. I tried other forms of the same thing – using periods (not allowed), dashes (not allowed), shortened it, but that was taken. I googled the name (why hadn't I done that before? Don't know). Found there is already a ministry with that name - a very cool one I might add. Instead of being discouraged I chose to consider it might be a teacher for me or a ministry for me to support. After investigating further I may support and/or get involved but their aim is not the same as mine. I looked into other options even googling another variation on the name I had only to find there are ministries with that too!! I was shocked. I was apparently naïve to think I was so original. But still with all the negativity coming at my mind *(JAB!)* I just kept going. I considered another name but THAT was taken also. But it was taken by another blogger. A very cool blog I might add. Hmm. Where do I go from here? I came up with a name and suitable tagline for the time. I have changed it since then. But the point is - I didn't lose anything – I accomplished what I set out to do and kept my peace. Glory to God.

New response noticed:

My husband was putting beans left over from dinner in a container to put in the refrigerator. He asked me if I thought it was big enough. I went hmmm perhaps. He said it was good enough for him. I said *"if it isn't you'll have to get a larger one and we'll have to wash that one."* Ding – epiphany. That would not have been how it went a while back. <u>Previously</u> I would have second guessed that, chosen a larger dish "just in case" to make sure. I would act to avoid the condemning inner voice that would scream *"how could you do that?" (JAB!) How could you be so stupid? (JAB!) What is wrong with you? (JAB!) You do not deserve to breathe (JAB!). You are worthless (JAB!).* Resulting in an internal firing squad where I'd have to "go outside and shoot myself" so to speak *(JAB!).* That "firing squad" has no right to exist. People make mistakes. It is not the end of the world. We are loved by **The Pursuer.**

Victory in expressing needs:

My husband was working out of town for a few months and he would come to visit for a weekend every other weekend. On his first weekend visit home we went to the Armada Fair with our daughter and her family. They came and picked us up in their van. Upon getting in the back of the van my grandson starts to move to the back so he can sit next to me – which is very usual. While he is moving I am asked if that is ok and my initial reaction is a yes because that is what I usually do so that is what I should do. But I do not feel in agreement with my answer – AND I SPEAK UP!! I changed my answer! I voiced that I really would rather sit next to my husband because he has been gone and I miss him. Fear presents itself but evaporates as my daughter validates my need and begins to explain to my five year old grandson who is quite distressed by this information. I voiced my feelings/need not knowing if it would be "allowed." To my joy it was. I also had an opportunity to share my feelings in a direct and gentle way to my grandson which validated his feelings without giving up my need. Glory to God!

Seemingly silly freedoms:

I got my sock wet by stepping in something – I changed them. My undies were uncomfortable – I changed them. Previously I would require myself to deal with it. But there is no law stating only one pair of socks a day. No law for only one pair of undies a day. May sound silly but it was a victory for me. I matter.

Spoke up to the one with the power:

I was in the Emergency Room with my mother in law. It was no fun at all. We were having difficulty getting her the attention that she needed. When we finally did get a doctor to come in to see her, the doctor was uncooperative, unhelpful and arrogant. I did not allow the doctor to behave this way. I questioned her course of action. She rudely asked if we wanted another doctor. I actually stated YES that I wanted another doctor! Doctors fall into that category of the ones with the power, the mighty I had bowed to before. We did get another doctor who took proper care of her. This was a ginormous victory.

Victory over severe fear (JAB!):

Buying tickets from a friend that needed to unload them, my husband and I had the opportunity to go to a Lion's football game in Detroit. I knew he would want to go. We left for the game later than we should have. When we arrived at the parking structure, it was full and we were not prepared for that. I started to feel anxious. We drove around looking for a place to park and finally parked somewhere but not really knowing where we were in relation to where we needed to go. I was feeling more anxious. We encountered a trolley that took us to the stadium. I relaxed some. Driving through streets congested with people and vehicles was not fun. When we got to the gate there were hordes of people there with some being aggressive. Before we could enter the stadium they searched us. Something else I was not prepared for. I had a lot of anxiety going on inside of me. After entering the building we needed to locate our seats. I was not very useful at this point. My husband led the way to our section. By the time we got there I was visibly shaken. I was afraid of all the people. I felt lost even though I was not. We found our seats. Sitting still I was able to relax some and enjoyed the game to some extent. After it was over the anxiety began again as we exited in a sea of people. We took quite a long time to find our car as we got lost. I was internally panic stricken. When we finally found our car and I sat down in the front seat safe I came unglued. Sick to my stomach, sobbing and shaking uncontrollably. The side effects of that affected me for the remainder of the day like some kind of drug. I needed to make that never happen again. Through study I came to learn of something called Ochlophobia – fear of crowds or mobs and social anxiety disorder. Although I had experienced them before this was the most severe reaction I had ever encountered. I had been familiar with a bible verse addressing fear but finding it in another version it was more helpful. It called the fear craven, cringing and fawning. I looked up the definition of those words and read about myself. I was embarrassed. The things I read stated this as something I'd have to deal with forever. I refused to believe them. I had gotten free from that sickness they said I'd have forever – there has to be a way to be free. I learned more about these things – causes etc. I read that bible verse over and over every day. It told me that the fear was Not from God and that God gave me power and a calm and well balanced mind instead. I wanted that calm well balanced mind.

Approximately two years later my husband was working out of town in Missouri and I went to go visit him. While I was there we were given the opportunity to go to a Ram's game in St. Louis with our nephew and his wife. We looked online for how to get there and he told us where they usually park. We were more prepared than last time. However the roads in Missouri we found difficult to navigate and due to roads being closed we ended up on the bridge to Illinois. We stopped on the side of the road to find out where we were and what our options were. We had to go out of our way more to get back to where we started. I was calm this entire time. After getting to where we planned to park we discovered they do not take credit cards which was how we had planned to pay for it. Now we are in line at the parking structure and we are five dollars short of what they are asking. We offer to pull through and turn around because we are unable to pay and there is a long line behind us. I'm still calm. She waved us through. Free parking! Then we had to find where in there to park. All the spots were taken. I asked for assistance from someone who worked there and was rudely directed to where we could find ample parking. We parked. I took a photo of where we were and we headed for the stadium not really knowing how to get there from where we ended up. I'm still calm. We went down the elevator and found ourselves inside a hotel. We found our way outside and asked for directions where we needed to walk through a casino and underground. I took a photo of the entrance when we emerged outside. We finally found our way to the stadium. Thankfully we had been already informed what was allowed and was not allowed in the stadium. We found our seats, got food and drinks and had a wonderful time. Upon leaving to find our car we found it without a problem and got home just fine. This football game was a blast. A stark difference to the first. What "they" say you cannot overcome I find you can with the help of **The Pursuer.**

14

~ Getting Wings ~

I LOVE analogies. They are pictures made of words. Being a visual learner that is very important if I am going to actually understand. I need the words to "draw me a picture." Understanding can be in levels. Multiple pictures bring more understanding. I have used the word picture of paint by numbers and microsurgery prep to help understand what the heck was I doing for those almost twenty years before we moved to Arizona. I have learned that change takes time. Greater change takes even longer. I have thought about baked on food, dried up milk or baby formula in a bottle or a dish from the dishwasher that has the food cooked on from the hot drying cycle. Running water alone will not succeed to get them clean. Those things need to soak and then running water might work. Or you may need to scrub or scrape. Or another picture is a ball of yarn all tangled. How long would that take to straighten out? And don't even get me started talking about untangling Christmas lights!

It is good to take note of something here. All of those examples have process in common. There is incremental progress. It is not black and white. It is not start and arrive at the finish. It's a journey.

I found a book to help me see this in a new light. The book is called *"Hope for the Flowers."* It's about two caterpillars looking for more. One gets tired and bored of all the eating part of being a caterpillar and tries to find more out of life. He asks other caterpillars but they don't listen, not really. He discovers what appears to be the answer and he climbs in. Not really knowing what he is doing and where he is going he is not happy. He meets the other caterpillar on this pile and they become friends. It is about their inner struggle to become what they were designed to be even though they don't know what that is. It's about the passion for freedom and the cost of change. It's about refusing to stay where you are when you know there is more even if you don't know how to get there. It's about how true lasting change happens in that place of aloneness. It's a good read.

Another thing I learned about the metamorphosis process of caterpillars to butterflies sounds a little gross. The caterpillar once inside the cocoon releases enzymes that dissolves its tissues – it digests itself. It dissolves everything in a soup except something call imaginal discs. These have been in the caterpillar all along and carry what is needed for the various parts of the mature butterfly (eyes, wings etc.). Some caterpillars even have tiny parts of the butterfly on them while they are still caterpillars although they are not readily visible. Once all the necessary parts are dissolved into this soup the discs begin the cell division to form the butterfly. When the change is complete some butterflies still carry parts of the caterpillar (muscles or sections of the nervous system). I found this amazing. Even the seemingly black and white change of the butterfly has grey. Reminds me of my puzzle piece identity. I am WE.

I have gotten where I am today by refusing to stay where I was. Change is something I have done over and over again. When I got married I vowed inwardly to not raise my kids how I was raised. When I was told I would be sick for the rest of my life I refused to accept that and pursued getting well. When my kids each asked me those pointed questions I sought the real answer. When **The Pursuer** asked me to leave the familiar again, I entered a new unknown. When **The Pursuer** said to me right after our return to Michigan "Do not fear your nakedness for I am your covering." I knew there was more to come. I had no idea how much.

When we lived in Arizona we became aware that we had been isolated by design, that **The Pursuer** had plans. So much was accomplished in us through that process that I did not expect the isolation to continue once we returned to Michigan, but it did. Things long buried needed to be addressed and that is done best in private. Like in a cocoon. And like the caterpillar digests itself I seemed to go through a similar process digesting my childhood. It was painful. Sometimes it seemed like silly "navel gazing." However, it was profitable. I entered my own pain in a new way and with assistance. Some things are now dissolved and some things still remain. There is much that is new.

In addition to digesting my childhood I found myself digesting my beliefs. This began out in Arizona, maybe even earlier. I discovered a difference between what I had decided to believe and what I actually did in some things. There were things I had made a conscious decision to believe but they would fail to produce what I was expecting. Like I was climbing that pile in *"Hope for the Flowers."*

I knew deciding to believe is a good thing. I had been trained in things called *"faith without works is dead"* and *"corresponding action."* So when I found myself in situations and I was engaging the *"corresponding action"* but the results were not forthcoming I found it confusing. I had also been trained in things called *"confessions"* and *"speaking to the mountain"* but my efforts would often fall flat. Something needed to change. Like the two caterpillars, I got off the pile.

The word "see" came into play. I began hearing about how God sees us and how we need to see how He sees. But then even just getting a look at or learning what He sees isn't enough. The word picture was presented using the movie *"The Princess Diaries"* and how she was a princess before she knew she was. How even after she heard she was a princess, she couldn't accept it. And even after she decided to believe the queen she still couldn't "see" herself as one. The movie laid out a very nice word picture of the process and the emotion and the struggle to believe what was a fact but felt so odd, so untrue. Believing in the heart takes time, takes convincing. She was always a princess but she did not always believe it. It wasn't until after she could bring herself to actually believe it and see herself as a princess, that she could partake of the things that went with it and make choices within that context.

It is like that with us. I know I have heard many wonderful things over the years about how God sees me and loves me. Sadly my perceptions of how I saw Him and how I saw myself clouded my view and therefore robbed me of what was mine. Even how I saw others got in the way. The childhood broken mirrors of parents, teachers, peers, religious leaders and bad experiences impaired my ability to see and understand. **The Pursuer** has a perfect mirror. It is gazing at Jesus, who He is and what all that means. Yet when we look into this mirror we see such a perfection and the LOVE that it is difficult to process because it looks too good to be true. Yet it is true so we have to learn to accept it. It is learning to see ourselves how He sees us. We belong to Him. He laid down His life, on purpose, intentionally, because He loves us. It is His desire for us to have the advantage in life. Because of Him we have been given the right to receive help from God. Our hearts argue with such wonderfulness.

In my struggle to truly believe and then accept the lavish LOVE of **The Pursuer** I did some study. I studied out the Bible verse Romans 5:17 because it was the primary one used by the minister I was learning from at the time. This guy was new to me, and so I was, as I have confessed many times – skeptical. This ended up working in my favor because my study led me to information that exceeded what I had been hearing and seeing. I learned a new term that I had trouble thinking was true in any situation let alone with God. The term is *"gratuitous contract."* It is a legal term for a binding contract that is made for the sole benefit of the person on the receiving end. The person making it does so without any promised benefit or advantage to them. It is a gift. So this verse tells us that because of one man's choice of betrayal against God that death controlled all of mankind – because of just one. It then goes on to say that *"much more"* anyone that receives the *"abundance of grace"* along with the *"gift of righteousness"* will rule, have power in life – by just one also! The one being Jesus Christ. So this verse tells us that because of the treason of one man (Adam) against God that death controlled all of mankind – because of just one. It goes on to say that *"much more"* those (us / anyone) that accept the *"abundance of grace"* along with the *"gift of righteousness"* will rule, have power in life by just one also. The one being Jesus Christ. We have been offered righteousness as a gift, a gratuity, a gratuitous contract.

He did this because He knew we were incapable of it and He loves us, LOVE is who He IS. His perfection exceeds our ability to even fathom let alone try to perform it. Self-effort is ludicrous. He desires relationship with us. He created us to love. This abundance of grace from God is not a reward for good behavior. Quite the contrary. It is not do good, get good / do bad, get bad. If that were true we'd all be screwed. And we were, until the knowledge of redemption was unveiled. That is what the gospel is supposed to be – good news. Jesus fulfilled ALL righteousness and offers it to us. **The Pursuer** says *"come to me, I have everything you need, allow me."* Yet the ego of mankind wants to go it alone, like a three year old crying I can do it myself. But the perfection of God is not something we are capable of and He always knew it. Grace was the plan all along. All the legalities were taken care of by Jesus. It is finished. We just need to see it. **The Pursuer** helped me come to see using a video of a song called *"See His Love."*

Seeing. Seeing is so important. I'm not talking about with our eyeballs. I'm talking about with our heart. Things have been painting pictures on our hearts all of our lives. Some of it true, some of it false, some of it good, some of it vile. Every one of us is different. Our lives flow from our hearts. That sounded like just words until I saw. Really saw. I had read numerous times about how out of the abundance of the heart the mouth speaks. I had heard numerous times about renewing my mind. I had heard numerous times about meditating on scriptures. Apparently I didn't really get it. It took seeing. It's not like I did nothing. I did lots. That became part of the problem, trusting my actions in the name of responsibility instead of trusting Jesus and what He had done. I hadn't really understood what He had accomplished. Faith is not something we do. Faith is something we Have, it is something that is built in our hearts.

So how did I build? I, did not. I, needed to learn and do something called – REST. Stare in the mirror of Jesus and allow Him to build His LOVE in me. **The Pursuer** leading me and I need to simply cooperate. Learn to trust. Like that sheep Jesus talked about finding and carrying. LET Him LOVE me. There may be many things I found myself doing but how I was going about it was the point. Am I motivated by love? Am I trying to learn or to earn? Am I stressing or resting? Am I joyfully engaged in relationship or dutifully performing? Grace.

I believe that what **The Pursuer** has to say is the most powerful thing any human can have anything to do with. By the breath of the creator we became living souls so it stands to reason that His words, which are carried by His breath would bring us life also. Although the primary source for what He may say may be found in the Bible I do not believe He speaks so narrowly. He has spoken to me through many avenues, like movies, songs, dreams, people etc. I have found He translates what He wants to say to us into words we can assimilate. He talks to me differently than He would talk to you. Remember that thing called social location? He knows where we are coming from. We are all different yet we are all His treasure. I don't believe He contradicts the Bible but I have also learned we don't always understand it properly and that I can talk with Him about it if I believe it sounds strange to me. With Him being the originator of the Bible I believe He knows it better than I do, or any scholar for that matter. I have never found Him to be afraid of my questions or my skepticism I have been the one with the fear and the skepticism *(JAB!)*.

Words are funny things. They can be like running water, active and effective. They can be empty through misunderstanding or misuse. They come in different languages. In English they can confuse by having different, or even opposite, meanings for the same word or same spelling of a word. The Bible tells us that words either kill or give life and that we have the power to choose. Only humans have that power, the power to choose what they say. I know many people do not think what they say matters. I disagree. People can say hurtful things and throw a *"just kidding"* after it and either it causes people to not trust what they say or it leaves a wound behind on the one who doesn't believe the footnoted apology. A single match can start a forest fire which leaves no evidence of the match that started it all. Likewise mindless words can be spoken that cause such extensive damage while the one who spoke them is long gone by the time it's fully cycled. Consider all the programs to stop bullying. What do bullies primarily use – words. They may use other things but words are definitely a major tool. I witnessed that with my name. When Bully #3 spewed those death filled words at me, I believed them and they carried a carnage. When I changed my name to turn things around my name carried vitality, energy and power. If bullies can produce so much negative power consider how much positive power we have available to us. Just think about the power of encouragement.

Although I believe what we say matters I find it irritating when someone says to me "don't say that!" and proceeds to tell me what I should be saying. I don't believe we have the right to police the words out of each other's mouths. What you choose to say is your decision. It's enough for me to pay attention and hear what is coming out of my mouth, which is evidence of what is going on inside of me. And I believe **The Pursuer** has ample grace for us. He knows the reasons, the causes. He is aware of why that is coming out of our mouth. He is more concerned with that – the heart of the matter. He loves us and he'll teach us whatever we need to know if we want Him to.

I have been taught and trained and retrained again on the power of what we say. God created the world with words! When I first heard that, fear *(JAB!)* got involved which only added to being afraid to speak up. Not good. Not accurate either. Once grace got involved good things followed. The "confessions" or "affirmations" or whatever you want to call them that I once did expecting them to bring about change in my life because I was speaking, I now do differently. I do have things I go over every day, speaking them out loud, but with the purpose of reprogramming my mind so that I see differently. My words are not magic. It's like I'm choosing what I want to think just like I would choose an outfit to wear. If it's cold out I choose something warm. If I struggle with believing God loves me I focus on Bible verses that feed what I have chosen to believe. What I see in the mirror of Jesus. I approach it from the standpoint of planting into my heart rather than sending it out into the airwaves. Then when I find myself in a situation where emotions are faster than thinking, in a situation that would profit from that good stuff I've been rehearsing, that information is in my heart and my mind grabs from that reservoir to find what it needs. I respond instead of react. The words that come out of my mouth at *that* time, I actually believe, therefore they are the ones that hold more power. Instead of frantically spewing scriptures from memory or trying to remember what it said in the Bible, or biting my tongue because I feel like saying something nasty, I can have the words fueled by **The Pursuer** come out effortlessly, because I planted them there and I have come to actually believe them.

I have come to fully believe this amazing LOVE **The Pursuer** has been persuading me of. There have been so many things in the way. Even after pointing out to me that I had been convinced He continues to show me more of Himself and identify things that had gotten in the way.

I read a book that revealed to me another broken mirror, forever changing my perspective called *"Pagan Christianity."* The authors warn you in the introduction that if you're not prepared to have your beliefs challenged to put the book down. Comparing it to the red pill in *"Alice in Wonderland"* and *"The Matrix"* they said that there would be no going back. They were correct. **The Pursuer** had prepared me quite efficiently. I had already been digesting what I believe. In it I found reasons for many things that had bothered me for such a long time but I never understood why. Things that the "good child" in me would never before have questioned. Because of it I will never see the organized church the same again and for that I am thankful.

Don't get me wrong, I am not against the organized church. There are very many great benefits to it! I am not in the least sorry for my participation in it. I have learned so much. My counselor called our dependence on it as we raised our children a "lean to." It was the main reason we had the stability that we had. We didn't know what we were doing and we were surrounded by a community, a family, to help us. However there are many inherent drawbacks as well simply because it is so organized. Paint by number pictures are organized. Masterpieces are elegantly free flowing. I would guess there are many churches that carry all of the drawbacks the book identifies without apology. Yet at the same time I know there are many that fight against the very drawbacks that are inherently in the organization. I believe they fight against it because the LOVE of **The Pursuer** in them is real. Some fight harder than others. I have witnessed this. His LOVE in them is real even though they may not do everything "right" in the opinion of whoever happens to be holding the yardstick. But then is that not displaying the very grace that **The Pursuer** is endeavoring to get us to believe? Even when **The**

Pursuer is obscured by whatever mankind does or doesn't do, He is still there. He calls out to each of us privately in our hearts.

A way to picture this is with a Dr. Seuss story. Ever heard of *"Horton Hears a Who?"* Horton is surprised by a voice he hears coming from a dust speck. Those of his peer group think he has flipped his lid, ridicule him and try to dispose of the dust speck. None of their behavior changes the fact that the voice Horton heard was real. They only stop their persecuting behavior when they hear for themselves. We humans are skeptical like that. Yet **The Pursuer**, who IS with us always will find a way for us to hear Him if that is what we want. He desires us to experience Him.

There is so much in life that we do not understand. Despite all our learning there is always more. It only harms us when we act as if we know it all or have it all together. I believe we live in a world of broken mirrors. Everywhere we look for identity, validation, encouragement etc., falls short. People fail. It is simply a fact. So then there are those that kick against that mentality by looking to the mirror of self, calling it independence or being self-sufficient. I see that mirror broken also. We are not islands, we cannot function alone. Psychology itself supports that. Relying on only ourselves has drawbacks because it produces insufficiency. We were born needy.

Babies are needy. That is an obvious fact. Everyone is aware that the baby cannot feed itself, clothe itself, change itself etc. But there is something that I think has been overlooked. Studies have been done that reveal that babies and even animals will die without love, without contact. Somehow the belief creeps in that this need for love and contact lessens or goes away when we become adults. We call it growing up and becoming mature. But in the dark, where no one else sees, we know better. We feel the need gnawing inside, unidentified. It's called lonely.

I believe lonely has a cure. You can't order it online. You can't take a pill. You can't will it away. It abides until it ceases to be, ceases to be alone. I believe this is one reason why sharing is so important. But even after sharing with someone else we go back to our alone-ness. This need reveals why it is important that someone is with us even if they can't change negative circumstances going on. Lonely is a horrible feeling. It can be felt in varying degrees. When I picture deep loneliness I see inconsolable sorrow and wailing. It made me think of hell. Hell is something people don't like to talk about. I know I don't. The way I have perceived it in the past was a punishment that I needed to do stuff to avoid. Could it possibly be loneliness is hell? It is our choice of disconnection? The only way I believe this thing called lonely leaves our lives is through knowing **The Pursuer** is with us. Not just knowing like information, but that "being convinced" kind of knowing. Then you know you are not alone, ever, even if it feels like it, you know better. Comforted instead of lonely.

There are many obstacles out there discouraging us to believe this connection is possible let alone needed. I believe the God who created us loves us unconditionally, no loopholes, no footnotes. I have come to the conclusion that this is the most important thing for us to know and believe. There are many other things we can learn that are helpful and profitable in life. But I have found that apart from having the deep heart and soul connection that validates our inherent worth those things fall short.

Humans are amazing. No other species is like us. Solomon who was the wisest man stated that God placed eternity in our hearts. I believe it. I also believe that when we look into that eternal mirror in our hearts without that love connection with **The Pursuer** we look upon a broken mirror. No discipline or behavior can bridge that. To see our value, our purpose and experience the elation and satisfaction we were born for we need God's eyes, His mirror. When He sees us He is looking at Jesus. Jesus reflects the perfection we need, we crave. When we have Him, we have everything. We don't have to have Him – it is our choice. We can choose to be separate from Him and He will let us even though it breaks His heart. LOVE is only real through intentional choice. We are sacred to our creator and I believe He has taken care of anything and everything we need. He chose us. What we choose is the kicker.

I choose **The Pursuer**. Even though it has taken me so long to see Him, really see Him and embrace Him, due to the various broken mirrors I was looking at. **The Pursuer** never left me. He pursues us like a suitor because we are His beloved. We don't understand His language because we are surrounded by broken mirrors that warp His voice. I reached for Him long before I understood and He has been there all along. Seeing through His eyes changes everything. My past does not define me. What other people say does not define me. My behavior does not define me. The one I am in awesome wonder of does. I matter. I am complete in Him. I feel like I have gotten wings although I am still learning how to use them. And that's ok because forever starts today and that is plenty of time to explore and learn the magnitude of His magnificence. Perhaps you would like to embark on a journey with **The Pursuer**, the Spirit of Grace. He's always been there, just look.

"Surely your goodness and unfailing love
will pursue me all the days of my life, and I will live
in the house of the Lord forever."

Psalm 23:6 (NLT)

15

Epilogue
ℰℛ

While I was writing this book I came across two other books. Two books I would never have read before. However **The Pursuer** brought them to my attention with that inner witness thing and so I acquired them, putting them aside to read after I was done writing my story.

One is called *"The Shack"* by William P Young. I explained why I had not read it before in chapter seven. I started it the day I completed writing this book. I was amazed over and over while reading it. I found myself putting it down in shock as I saw overlap in my story and his. Not the same, just that sharing overlap. A different view of the same **Pursuer.** Perfect timing. **The Pursuer** is wise.

The other is *"Waking Up in Heaven"* by Crystal McVea and Alex Tresniowski. Previously I had a very strong aversion to any stories people had of going to heaven or hell. Previously I had been afraid. I am no longer afraid. I am only half way through this now and have put it down numerous times in absolute shock and awe of the overlap. Again, not the same, just that sharing overlap. A different view of the same **Pursuer.**

So why would you care, why do I tell you? I tell you to encourage you to encounter overlap, to share with others, to find your puzzle pieces, to see **The Pursuer** from your view. I have included a resource section for you to pick and choose things that may assist you. Of course it is not an exhaustive list. The world is full of resources. And, you most likely will not like all of them. Some things you might like just parts of, like that book I told you I read & then threw away after getting a nugget I needed. I myself don't like every part of everything on my list. People are involved and we are inaccurate and/or in process. I encourage you to not be afraid to explore. Take what you like, ignore what you choose, allow one thing to lead you to another. It is your life. It is your choice. Being intentional is a great tool and **The Pursuer** is an excellent guide. My greatest wish for you is to come to know the safe rest and elegant leading found in **The Pursuer** who loves YOU no matter where you are in your journey.

16

❧RESOURCES❧

<u>QR Code Web Addresses</u>
(In the order they appear in the book)

Where you can find the answer to *"What is a QR code?"*
http://goo.gl/F1wM4n

"There's a Hole in my Sidewalk" by Portia Nelson
http://goo.gl/WabMIz

Lyrics to *"Whatever You're Doing (Something Heavenly)"* by Sanctus Real
http://goo.gl/xUZGhN

Details on the historic FBI Miami shootout
http://goo.gl/LHxkx

Short video clip of *Darmok* episode showing the inability to communicate and subsequent frustration it caused.
http://goo.gl/dlPdwM

Short video clip of *Darmok* episode showing the sharing and subsequent understanding that follows.
http://goo.gl/YckBIU

Portion of the script from *"The Neverending Story"* where Bastian and Atreau become aware of each other and their reactions.
http://goo.gl/bL7IVw

Short video clip of *Innerlight* episode showing what the captain retained from the sharing.
http://goo.gl/kB3MB7

Dissertation on *Social Location* by Dr. David Rhoads
http://goo.gl/5aOj44

"Effect Of Traumatic Events On Children" by Bruce D Perry, MD, Ph.D.
http://goo.gl/TqxH9n

"Loneliness Is More Dangerous Than We Thought" article by Beth Greenfield
http://goo.gl/7AjUZT or http://goo.gl/W8KpBr

Untitled poem by Aaron Sorkin illustrating that true help comes from truly sharing.
http://goo.gl/JgwGeB

Helpful Websites

You Matter website
http://goo.gl/XMUHB9

Trauma Articles – Psych Central (multiple authors)
http://goo.gl/J0ki8i

Emotional Abuse – American Humane Association
http://goo.gl/qSauP4

Signs of Emotional Abuse by Maria Bogdanos – Psych Central
http://goo.gl/HvS9K

Emerging From Broken: From Surviving to Thriving on the Journey to Wholeness – Darlene Ouimet
http://goo.gl/3g6n1

For Adult Survivors of Emotional Child Abuse – The Invisible Scar
http://goo.gl/BHykRI

You Can NOT Be Replaced website
http://goo.gl/ms2PT2

Reading Material

Battlefield Of The Mind *(Joyce Meyer)*
Beauty For Ashes *(Joyce Meyer)*
Emerging From Broken: The Beginning of Hope for Emotional Healing *(Darlene Ouimet)*
Healing Grief *(Amy Hillyard Jensen)*
Hope for the Flowers *(Trina Paulua)*
Loving Our Kids On Purpose: Making A Heart To Heart Connection *(Danny Silk)*
Overcoming Offenses *(David G Huskey with Linda Thaxton Hill)*
Pagan Christianity *(Frank Viola and George Barna)*
The Bible – *any and all translations that help*
The Blessing Of The Lord: Makes Rich And He Adds No Sorrow With It *(Kenneth Copeland)*

The Power of Your Words *(Don Gossett and E. W. Kenyon)*
The Shack *(William P Young)*
The Tree That Survived The Winter *(Mary Fahy)*
The Wall: A Parable *(Gloria Jay Evans)*
What to Say When You Talk to Yourself *(Shad Helmstetter, PhD)*

Other Reading

(Life) John 10:10 in The Message translation
(Love) I John 3:1, 4:10, 18, 19 in the Good News Translation
(Mirror) II Corinthians 3:18 in the Amplified Bible
John chapter 14-17 in multiple translations (read out loud)

Songs

You can search online for the lyrics and then buy them online if you like. Or if you are visual like I am you will find lyric videos found online more helpful than just listening. Whatever works for you!

All of Creation by MercyMe
Always by Kristian Stanfill
Amazed by Lincoln Brewster
Anthem by Jesus Culture
Anyway by Nichole Nordeman
Be Loved by Christy Nockels
Beautiful the Blood by Steve Fee
Beauty of Grace by Krystal Meyers
Brave by Gavin Mikhail
Brave by Sara Bareilles
Breath of Heaven by Amy Grant
Breathe by Matt Brouwer
Cornerstone by Hillsong
Forever Reign by Hillsong

Honesty by Margaret Becker

How Great Thou Art – all four verses

I Am New by Jason Gray

I Know Who I Am by Israel and New Breed

I Will Carry You by Michael W Smith

In Your Presence by Brian and Jenn Johnson

It's Your Blood by Steve Chalmers

Just Come In by Margaret Becker

Keep Holding On by Avril Lavigne

Love Me by JJ Heller

More Like Falling In Love by Jason Gray

My Beloved by Kari Jobe

No Sweeter Name by Kari Jobe

Not For A Moment by Meredith Andrews

Nothing Ever (Could Separate Us) by Citizen Way

Nothing Is Impossible by Planetshakers

O Taste and See by Jenn and Brian Johnson

O The Blood by Gateway Worship

Our God by Chris Tomlin

One Thing Remains by Kristian Stanfill

Power of Love by Celine Dion

Power of Your Love by Worth Dying For

Reach by Peter Furler

Remain by Royal Tailor

Rise by Shawn McDonald

Rooftops by Jesus Culture

Safe by Phil Wickham

Sanctuary Me by Chris Rodriguez

See His Love by Jesus Culture

The More I Seek You by Gateway/Kari Jobe

The Proof of Your Love by For King and Country
This is What You Do by Bethel Music
True Colors by Cyndi Lauper
We Are Free by Aaron Shust
Wind Beneath My Wings by Better Midler
Wrap Me in Your Arms by Michael Gungor
You Never Let Go by Matt Redman
Your Great Name by Natalie Grant
Your Love oh Lord by Third Day

Made in the USA
Charleston, SC
06 November 2014